Journal Like a Stoic

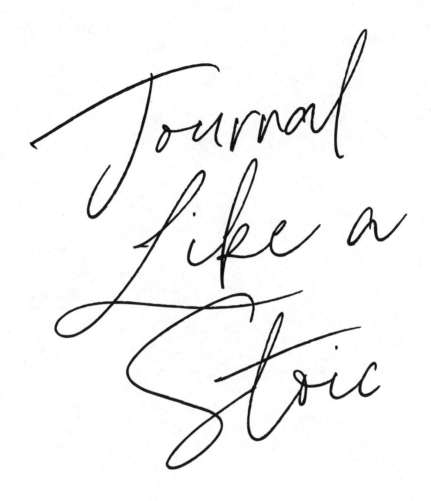

Journal Like a Stoic

A 90-Day Stoicism Program to
Live with Greater Acceptance, Less
Judgment, and Deeper Intentionality

BRITTANY POLAT, PhD

Zeitgeist • New York

Published in the United States by Zeitgeist, an imprint of Zeitgeist™,
a division of Penguin Random House LLC, New York.

penguinrandomhouse.com

Zeitgeist™ is a trademark of Penguin Random House LLC

ISBN: 9780593435892

Author photograph © by Keni Parks

Illustration © clu/DigitalVision Vectors via Getty Images

Book design by Aimee Fleck

Edited by Erin Nelson

Printed in the United States of America

1 3 5 7 9 10 8 6 4 2

First Edition

CONTENTS

Introduction • 11

PART I
UNDERSTANDING STOIC PHILOSOPHY 17

PART II
THE STOIC WAY OF LIFE 29

COURSE A

EXAMINING THE INNER CRITIC

DAY 1: Opening Your Mind • 32

DAY 2: Seeking Truth • 34

DAY 3: Finding Quiet Courage • 36

DAY 4: Your Essential Nature • 38

DAY 5: Your Internal Compass • 40

DAY 6: Filtering the Nonessential • 42

DAY 7: Respecting Your Essence • 44

DAY 8: A Second Look at Judgment • 46

DAY 9: Between Stimulus and Response • 48

DAY 10: Befriending Yourself • 50

DAY 11: Tightening Values • 52

DAY 12: Calming Your Nervous System • 54

DAY 13: Wrestling with Restlessness • 56

DAY 14: A Closer Look at Your Gifts • 58

DAY 15: Have You Met Me? • 60

DAY 16: From Foe to Friend • 62

DAY 17: Your Inner Citadel • 64

DAY 18: The Same Standard of Forgiveness • 66

DAY 19: Goodbye, External Validation • 68

DAY 20: A Humble Storefront • 70

DAY 21: Staying on the Path • 72

DAY 22: Finding Your Genius • 74

DAY 23: Lighting Your Inner Flame • 76

DAY 24: Swapping Pity for Productiveness • 78

DAY 25: Your Internal Applause • 80

DAY 26: The Anxiety Antidote • 82

DAY 27: Keeping Things Simple • 84

DAY 28: Sticking to Your Story • 86

DAY 29: It's Your Life to Live • 88

DAY 30: Time for Your Fig • 90

COURSE B

THE ROAD TO ACCEPTANCE

DAY 31: No Time Like Right Now • 94

DAY 32: Changing Your Mind • 96

DAY 33: To React or Not to React? • 98

DAY 34: Curbing the Consumption Craving • 100

DAY 35: Dealing with Imperfect Humans • 102

DAY 36: Respect in Disagreement • 104

DAY 37: The Art of Preparedness • 106

DAY 38: Building Good Habits • 108

DAY 39: Using Your Resources • 110

DAY 40: Accepting Constant Change • 112

DAY 41: Living in Harsh Conditions • 114

DAY 42: The Good Within • 116

DAY 43: Intention over Outcome • 118

DAY 44: Life's Rhythms • 120

DAY 45: Facing Solitude or a Crowd • 122

DAY 46: Bearing Misfortune Nobly • 124

DAY 47: Which Handle Will You Hold? • 126

DAY 48: Living by Example • 128

DAY 49: What If It Were Gone? • 130

DAY 50: Eating Some Dirt • 132

DAY 51: Accountability Check • 134

DAY 52: Taming Your Temper • 136

DAY 53: In Their Shoes • 138

DAY 54: Trusting the Helm • 140

DAY 55: One Thing We
Know for Sure • 142

DAY 56: A Beautiful Loan • 144

DAY 57: Virtue as a Mainstay • 146

DAY 58: Celebration and
Recovery • 148

DAY 59: An Indivisible Point • 150

DAY 60: Unbroken Calm
and Freedom • 152

COURSE C
LIVING WITH VIRTUE

DAY 61: From Reaction
to Intention • 156

DAY 62: The Art of Living • 158

DAY 63: A Disciplined Artist • 160

DAY 64: Your Daily Mindset • 162

DAY 65: Like an Emerald • 164

DAY 66: Seeing Problems
at Scale • 166

DAY 67: The Power of Choice • 168

DAY 68: Web of Compassion • 170

DAY 69: Cross-Examining
Judgment • 172

DAY 70: To Adapt Is to Love • 174

DAY 71: A Second Look
at Desire • 176

DAY 72: Testing Your Resolve • 178

DAY 73: The Busy Barometer • 180

DAY 74: Maintaining
Attention • 182

DAY 75: Natural State of
Kindness • 184

DAY 76: Compassion as
Justice • 186

DAY 77: Context Is
Everything • 188

DAY 78: Identifying Role
Models • 190

DAY 79: The Cost of Greed • 192

DAY 80: Integrity Without
Fanfare • 194

DAY 81: Making Your
Own Luck • 196

DAY 82: What Rules You? • 198

DAY 83: Cultivating
Gratitude • 200

DAY 84: Delight in Your
Companions • 202

DAY 85: Finding Your Flow • 204

DAY 86: Making the Most
of Mistakes • 206

DAY 87: Don't Overdo It • 208

DAY 88: A Soul Retreat • 210

DAY 89: Self-Reflection as
Daily Practice • 212

DAY 90: Replenishing the
Good Within • 214

Closing Words • 217
Acknowledgments • 219
References • 220

Philosophy molds and constructs the soul; it orders our life, guides our conduct, shows us what we should do and what we should leave undone; it sits at the helm and directs our course as we waver amid uncertainties. Without it, no one can live fearlessly or in peace of mind. Countless things that happen every hour call for advice; and such advice is to be sought in philosophy.

—

Seneca, *Moral Letters to Lucilius*, 16.3

INTRODUCTION

The day before I left home for college, I visited my grandmother for a farewell hug. With her characteristic wit, she offered parting words of advice: "If someone tries to sell you magic beans, don't buy them!" I laughed, wondering what she meant—surely magic beans were for fairy tales?—but I thought about those words often after I left home.

I thought I would find happiness by living in a certain place, looking a certain way, or having a certain job. But every time I achieved these external successes, happiness slipped through my fingers. I came to realize there are no magical cure-alls for our problems. I learned through experience that if someone or something promises us the world, we should be skeptical. Over time, I learned we get the most out of life when we put in hard work and exercise good judgment.

When I discovered Stoicism some 15 years later, I couldn't help but think of my grandmother. Was this just an ancient version of magic beans? I was looking for answers about how to navigate a difficult time in my life—changing careers, relocating to a new state, and raising three energetic young children. I searched the web for "books on wisdom" and stumbled upon William B. Irvine's *A Guide to the Good Life: The Ancient Art of Stoic Joy*. What was Stoic joy?

My interest was piqued. I found many more books making huge promises about Stoicism: wisdom, happiness, and tranquility would be mine if I could wrap my head around this 2,000-year-old philosophy. It seemed too good to be true. Still, I ordered the books and kept an open mind.

As I read more about Stoicism, I realized that it isn't a self-help fairy tale. It's a deeply thoughtful, firmly rooted system for living a good life. Stoicism has a long history of helping people make sense of their lives and endure hardship. In fact, it has been a tried-and-true method for crafting a life with purpose and intention for over two millennia. In a way, it's the opposite of magic beans. Living by Stoic principles takes discipline and introspection. In other words: it's hard work.

To get something out of this process, you need to put a lot into it. That's why this course provides 90 days of lessons and intensive journaling work for you. The work is not for naught: research shows that people who practice Stoicism have reduced negative emotions and a greater sense of vigor in their lives. I certainly experienced those benefits for myself as I continued to practice and grow as a Stoic. I read every book on Stoicism I could get my hands on. I started a website, wrote my first book on Stoicism and parenting, and jumped into the worldwide Stoic community. Later I began working with Modern Stoicism and the Stoic Fellowship, two nonprofits that promote Stoicism all over the world. More recently, I've started a new nonprofit called Stoicare, which focuses on Stoic wisdom, well-being, community, and care.

At its best, Stoicism offers stable, sturdy roots for finding acceptance and contentment in your life. But here's the thing: only you can think deeply about what it is you want and decide how to live accordingly. Living with peace and purpose is an inside job. No magic beans necessary.

HOW TO USE THIS JOURNAL

This journal course consists of two parts: background information on Stoicism and 90 days of journaling with the help of Stoic quotes. In part I, you'll learn about the core principles and history of Stoicism. We'll meet the historical figures whose advice will carry you throughout the course, and you'll get a sense of why Stoicism is a practical life philosophy.

In part II, you'll begin exploring Stoic ideas for yourself. Each day, we'll review a nugget of ancient wisdom, followed by a lesson that contextualizes this advice for contemporary challenges. You'll have a chance to reflect deeply on the meaning of each Stoic lesson, journaling about its applications in your own life.

All the courses align with a core element of daily Stoic practice. They look like this:

COURSE A: EXAMINING THE INNER CRITIC asks you to cultivate clarity and courage as you develop a healthier relationship with your own mind.

COURSE B: THE ROAD TO ACCEPTANCE helps you fully embrace your life, adapt to new challenges, and discover profound acceptance of our beautiful, unpredictable world.

COURSE C: LIVING WITH VIRTUE bolsters your newfound wisdom with a greater sense of purpose and peace, tapping into your inner capacity for strength and kindness.

By the end of your 90-day journaling experience, you'll be well on your way to living with less judgment, more intention, and greater acceptance. What's more, you'll have the tools you need to continue exploring Stoic ideas on your own, both in theory and in real-life practice.

JOURNALING TIPS

PROCEED IN ORDER

The courses have been specially designed to progress from straightforward lessons at the beginning to more complex lessons toward the end. All these prompts will inspire deep reflection, but the earlier lessons will prepare you for the more demanding inquiry later on. My recommendation is to tackle these chronologically.

BE CONSISTENT

Try to make journaling a part of your daily routine and lifestyle. Ideally, you'll find a consistent time and place to journal every day, or at least several times a week. If this isn't possible, just work with what you've got. But remember, the more consistently you journal, the more impact you'll see in your daily life. (If possible, write with the same pen every day. This adds a dash of consistency to the writing process when other variables, like time and place, are hard to control.)

FILL YOUR PAGES

I encourage you to make full use of the space provided in this journal—it will serve as a physical record of your psychological and spiritual growth. If you need to use an additional journal as overflow space, go right ahead. Keep in mind, though, that we're not aiming for length, but for reflective depth and introspective insight. What matters is not word count but your commitment to the journaling process.

CREATE A JOURNALING PRACTICE

For best results, create a ritual around your journaling routine. This will help prepare your mind for serious introspection and make journaling pleasant and beneficial. Find a peaceful spot that allows for quiet reflection and consider bringing along a cup of coffee, tea, or water to get your thoughts flowing.

PART I

Understanding Stoic Philosophy

In part I, we'll explore the origins and foundational ideas behind Stoic philosophy. You'll learn about the shipwreck that led to a philosophical revolution. You'll understand how practicing the four virtues can create space for clarity, confidence, and contentment. And we'll see why the most powerful person on Earth studied the words of a humble former slave. By the end of this section, it will be clear why Stoicism is a philosophy for *everyone*, and you'll be ready to try it out for yourself.

THE STOIC UNIVERSE

Stoicism is a philosophy of life in the fullest sense. As a framework for daily living, it can guide us in every decision we make, from our career choices to what's for dinner tonight. What's more, it helps ground us when we're living through what feels like unprecedented times.

Through its three interrelated disciplines of logic, ethics, and physics, Stoicism helps us understand our relationship to ourselves, the cosmos, and other people. Stoicism allows us to understand our purpose and our path in a way that few other philosophies can, because it draws us back to our inner riches and urges us to focus on what we can control. Let's look briefly at these three disciplines and how they can help us live a good life today.

LOGIC

How do we know what is true and what isn't? What is the best way to debate a topic? These were some of the questions the ancient Stoics asked and answered. Stoic logic covered many of our rational thinking activities.

Today, logic is as important as ever. We don't want to be deluded about the world around us or mistakenly believe that false things are true. For example, if you read an article on how to have the best sleep of your life, how do you know if it's true? If an impulsive idea pops into your mind—*I need to buy new kitchen gear*—how do you decide whether it's a good idea? Stoic logic helps us evaluate propositions made by others and propositions we form in our own minds. It enables us to think clearly and accurately about the world so we can make wise decisions that serve our principles and goals.

ETHICS

The Stoics built their ethics around the belief that humans are rational and social. We find our greatest happiness when we successfully interact with other people. To the Stoics, that meant showing patience, kindness, and tolerance even when other people do not. Stoicism teaches us how to deal with all kinds of people—even those who are selfish, frustrating, or otherwise misguided—while still preserving our inner peace and freedom.

PHYSICS

In ancient Stoicism, "physics" referred to the study of the natural world and the cosmos. The Stoics believed the universe is imbued with a divine spirit (pneuma) and that humans, animals, plants, and the Earth—everything under the sun—share in this divine cohesion.

As you read ancient Stoic texts, you will encounter many beautiful and moving references to cosmic nature. Some Stoics today share the ancient belief that nature is divine, rational, and providential. Other Stoics prefer to interpret these passages metaphorically, reading them as statements on the interconnectedness of all things. Whether you choose to interpret Stoic nature as divine or not, I encourage you to cultivate the sense of awe, wonder, and gratitude that flows from the contemplation of the natural world.

THE FOUR VIRTUES OF STOICISM

What makes a good life? The ancient Stoics believed the answer is *virtue*, or inner excellence. When we focus on building up our inner resources—our mindset, character, and moral choices—we activate a deep, rich, and long-lasting happiness. No matter what craziness is happening around us, we can find peace and purpose through virtuous action. While it takes time and training to build up to this ideal, it's something we can all achieve with patience and hard work.

Far from being dull or restrictive, virtue represents the pinnacle of human achievement. Each one of us has the potential to bring out the best in our nature by cultivating the following four primary virtues.

WISDOM

We all face choices in life, and wisdom helps us make decisions that reflect our deepest aspirations and intentions. Wisdom shows us what's important, what's worth fighting for, and when we should step back or let go. Wisdom challenges us to look deeper into the nature of things, to see past surface appearances and focus our limited time and energy on meaningful projects.

JUSTICE

In the Stoic context, justice refers to how we treat other people. Do we treat others with respect and set a good example? Do we understand that no one person (including ourselves) is more important than another? When led by the principle of justice, our attitudes and actions are fair and evenhanded, even generous, and benevolent when appropriate. Justice helps remove the overreactive, self-centered, or biased component of our interactions with others, enabling us to focus less on ourselves and more on the collective human experience. Through Stoicism, we learn to care more deeply about others, from our dearest friends to people on the other side of the world.

COURAGE

Stoic courage involves training our mind, body, and spirit to endure difficulty. As one ancient source put it, "Courage concerns instances of standing firm." Do we have what it takes to overcome challenges, even when it's hard? Do we persevere through hardship, take on demanding tasks when required, and stand by our beliefs even when no one supports us? For Stoics, when we move closer to these questions, we begin to live courageously.

TEMPERANCE

The idea behind temperance is to control our impulses, keeping them within reasonable bounds. When guided by temperance, we shift our desires away from superficial temptations (physical pleasure, money, power, fame) and move toward inner riches that promote long-term flourishing (self-discipline and skillful patience). Temperance is not about giving up all your pleasures in life; it's about finding an even greater joy in those things that are truly valuable, like being an ethical and honorable person.

THE ORIGINS OF STOICISM

In ancient Greece, classical Athens (fifth and fourth centuries BCE) was a philosophical Wild West, with people peddling ideas about the fundamental questions of the world on every street corner. Philosophers gathered in public spaces to debate and borrow ideas from one another, setting off a chain reaction of philosophical innovation for the next several hundred years. To name just one noteworthy set of influencers, Socrates tutored Plato, who mentored Aristotle, each forming his own philosophical school of thought along the way.

This era of inspiration gave way to the Hellenistic Period, during which philosophers debated the best path to *eudaimonia*, or flourishing happiness. It was against this backdrop of deep inquiry and public debate that Zeno of Citium formed the doctrine of Stoicism around 300 BCE. Its name comes from the Stoa Poikile, or Painted Porch, where Zeno was fond of lecturing.

Unlike his peers, Zeno taught that virtue was necessary and sufficient for happiness. In other words, regardless of our material conditions, we could live a satisfying life if we had a virtuous character. Highly respected in Athens, Zeno gathered many devoted followers over his lifetime. Despite the fact that there is very little record of Zeno's original writings, scholars have been able to piece together his ideas from the Greek Stoa, or early Stoic tradition, to provide us with a template.

What can we glean from this framework? Stoics were unique in their insistence that good character is all we need to live a good life. This pragmatism later appealed to the Romans (who conquered Greece) as they adopted Stoicism's teachings and propagated its way of life, giving rise to some of the most famous Stoics we refer to today.

STOIC THINKERS

From Zeno to Marcus Aurelius, Stoics have tried to live with virtue and distinction. Those drawn to Stoicism are often inquisitive, committed, highly principled, and deeply pragmatic while remaining reflective. Knowing a bit about the famous historical Stoics provides important context for part II, in which we'll put these principles into practice. Let's take a deeper look at Stoicism's emergence in Athens and its dissemination around the map.

THE ORIGINAL STOIC MIND

Zeno of Citium, originally from the Mediterranean island of Cyprus, was a merchant who traded valuable goods under the Greek empire.

As the story goes, on one voyage, Zeno's ship sank and he lost everything. Distraught and empty-handed, Zeno sought refuge at a bookstore in Athens, where he picked up a volume on the life of Socrates. Enthralled with Socrates' bold philosophy, he asked the bookseller, "Where can I find a man like this?" The bookseller pointed to a passing philosopher named Crates and said, "Follow him."

Now, we can't be completely sure this is how Zeno came to philosophy (although it makes for a great founding myth), but we do know he spent several years studying at philosophical schools around Athens. Eventually Zeno started lecturing near the public marketplace, inspiring many from the Painted Porch.

Zeno's philosophical legacy can be summed up by his pithy goal for life: "Live in agreement with nature." The Stoic school he founded made major advances in subjects like propositional logic (still used by your computer today) and psychology (still used by *you* today). When Zeno died, he was honored by the Athenians with a public tomb and an inscription praising his contributions to their city.

THE NEXT WAVE OF STOICS

After Zeno, leadership of the Stoa passed into the hands of Cleanthes of Assos. Cleanthes had been a boxer in his youth, and he paid for his philosophical training by working as a water carrier. Known for his piety, Cleanthes oversaw the school while "followers of the porch" debated how to interpret and apply Zeno's doctrines.

Next came Chrysippus of Soli, who authored treatises, or philosophical essays, and formalized the school's positions on epistemology, physics, and logic. The logic of the Stoicism we know today was systematized by Chrysippus. He was so brilliant and influential that one later historian noted, "If there had been no Chrysippus, there would have been no Stoa."

The Stoic school was led by a succession of scholars until the Roman takeover, when it was disbanded as a formal institution. But Stoicism remained popular, and during the Roman imperial period it regained prominence. Stoics like Hecato of Rhodes continued writing, while others, like Musonius Rufus, taught, tutored, and influenced courts through Stoicism.

Most of the ancient Stoic writings that have come down to us today are from the Roman imperial period. What we have from Seneca, Epictetus, and Marcus Aurelius are not academic papers but personal letters, diaries, and lectures. They're the words of real people grappling with real-world problems.

Seneca and Epictetus

Seneca—wealthy statesman, playwright, and tutor to the young emperor Nero—saw his fair share of human weakness at the imperial court. Before Nero came of age, Seneca successfully helped him run the Roman Empire. But even a Stoic couldn't rein in Nero for long. Nero's violent tendencies came to the fore as he executed political rivals, had his own mother assassinated, and demonstrated a penchant for unusual cruelty to both friend and foe.

Nero eventually tired of Seneca's influence and ordered him to commit suicide. Seneca made a grand philosophical exit, discoursing on virtue to his friends and preventing his weeping wife from following him to the grave. Unfortunately, his reputation was tarnished by his willingness to indulge some of Nero's bad behavior. Today, Seneca is considered one of the most complex (or compromised) of the ancient Stoics.

His flaws notwithstanding, Seneca's works are considered some of the best sources of ancient Stoic advice. In the form of plays, essays, and letters, Seneca spoke to universal problems: anger, money, friendship, and the passage of time. In Seneca's writing, we catch a glimpse of ourselves—not perfect, but always trying to improve.

In contrast, Epictetus was the sagelike teacher who lived a simple life far away from the glittering power center of Rome. While born into slavery, he was able to study Stoic philosophy with Musonius Rufus. When eventually granted freedom, he went on to found his own philosophical school. Although he left no written works, one of his students, Arrian, circulated notes from Epictetus' discussions. These notes (known as the *Discourses* and the *Handbook*) became famous and are all that remain of his teachings.

From the *Discourses*, it's clear why so many looked up to Epictetus: his straight-talking lessons punctured inflated egos and set his students on a clearer path to wisdom. He cracked jokes at his own expense, thundered at hypocrites, and committed himself to exploring inner freedom. His mind left a lasting impact on all who studied Stoicism after him, including renowned philosopher-emperor Marcus Aurelius.

Marcus Aurelius

Marcus Aurelius is the pinnacle of ancient political power and popular philosophical influence. As Roman emperor, he was the most powerful man on Earth, with vast riches and legions of soldiers at his disposal. Yet Marcus tried to live like a philosopher. He made wise policy decisions, treated others with consideration, curbed his desire for luxuries, and made peace with his impending death. Marcus struggled with others' disloyalty, but he devoted his life to the public.

And, like any human, Marcus led a life full of triumph and tragedy. Many of his children died in infancy; he constantly dealt with barbarian invasions and military revolts; and he lived through one of the worst plagues in European history. He wrote at least part of the *Meditations*—a private philosophical journal—while on a difficult military campaign.

Through this personal notebook, Marcus found comfort in repeating and reaffirming his Stoic principles. His poetic sensibility and philosophical commitment have inspired generations of leaders and thinkers, making the *Meditations* one of the most-read books of all time.

STOICISM IS FOR EVERYONE

In ancient Greece and Rome, many everyday people—women, the enslaved, and poor individuals—were barred from philosophical communities. Worse, they were excluded from politics and brutalized in society. At best, disenfranchised individuals were invited in only when wealthy men decided to open the doors.

Historians believe that while Stoicism was constrained by these cultural practices, it was nonetheless more inclusive than other philosophical creeds at the time. Many early Stoics believed that virtue was available to everyone, including people living through poverty or political oppression. (Recall that the great Stoic teacher Epictetus was a former slave.) Many Stoics even advocated for women to receive formal philosophical training.

While today it feels trite to applaud such limited access, to explore the history of Stoicism (and much of history, really) is to confront these shameful truths. It can be difficult, even discouraging, to contextualize ancient cultural practices. Yet it's my belief, as a woman who might have been left out of many early Stoic debates, that there is still much to learn from this deeply reflective philosophy that has guided humans from many backgrounds for over 2,000 years. Much of the world agrees.

Stoic philosophy is not confined to one culture group or life experience. Today, it is practiced all over the globe by a diverse array of people. There are thriving Stoic communities on six continents, in dozens of countries, and in multiple languages. Stoicism speaks to a universal human experience, providing tools for all of us to live with greater intention, purpose, and acceptance.

When we update and adapt Stoicism for our time, we find virtue, truth, progress, and the potential of every person to cultivate their highest human nature. That's why I continue to study and practice Stoicism, with a few modifications. When I read original Stoic texts, I replace the pronouns in my head so that they have a more universal applicability. We've adapted the texts here to be more inclusive. No matter your story or background, I encourage you to develop your own method for relating Stoicism to your daily life.

STOIC SPOTLIGHT

Perhaps the most influential historical woman to make her mark on Stoicism was Elizabeth Carter, the first person to translate Epictetus' *Discourses* into English. Carter, a self-taught polyglot and writer, was known for her upstanding character as well as her scholarship. In eighteenth-century England, when women were expected to marry young and start running a household, Carter refused several offers of marriage to become an internationally respected scholar.

Carter was highly esteemed by literary luminaries like Samuel Johnson, who created the first comprehensive English dictionary, and was friends with other accomplished women of the era. Her translations of the *Discourses* and the *Handbook* remained the English standard for over a century. Although Elizabeth Carter did not refer to herself as a Stoic, she exemplified the wisdom, knowledge, and personal excellence of Stoic leaders.

PART II

The Stoic Way of Life

Welcome to the journaling portion of this experience (i.e., your inner work). For every lesson, or day of journaling, there is a quote from an ancient Stoic, a brief reflection on this quote, and several writing prompts to help you root into your own inquiry. *Choose any one of the prompts* or tackle them all if you are feeling inspired. If you select one, the others will be there for you whenever you would like to exercise your journaling practice.

Plan for at least 10 to 15 minutes of reflection, trying your best to write (even just a little bit) each time you sit with the journal. It's okay if you need to take a break, but get back into your groove as soon as possible. The more intentional you are with your practice, and the longer you stick with it, the more likely you are to align your actions with your values, curb judgment in all forms, and settle into a life of inner tranquility.

EXAMINING THE INNER CRITIC

For the first 30 days, our focus will be your relationship with your*self*. We'll begin by sharpening awareness around your thoughts, releasing attachment to unhelpful judgments, and curbing self-criticism. You'll learn how to deepen self-compassion, practice humility, and avoid dependence on other people's opinions.

Remember, you don't need to complete both prompts: choose whichever one gets you closer to your desired outcome. Perhaps this is the prompt that stretches you more. By the end of 30 days, you'll understand how mental clarity and self-respect lead to self-acceptance and inner peace.

DAY 1: OPENING YOUR MIND

What is the first business of one who practices philosophy?
To get rid of thinking that one knows; for it is impossible
to get a human to begin to learn that which they think
they know.

Epictetus, *Discourses*, 2.17, 1

To live a good life, Epictetus says our first job is to see the world clearly, with fresh eyes. We learn to question our assumptions and ask ourselves whether our habitual thought processes are healthy and accurate. Our greatest asset during this process is an open mind. If you are open to making new discoveries about yourself and the world, you *will* make new discoveries.

1. Which of your old mental habits are no longer serving you? (Do you have a habit of negative self-talk? Do you tend to shy away from certain thoughts or feelings?)
2. Identify three things you would like to change about your mental habits.

• One of my mental habits (old ones) is to seek validation
  from others. I like challenges but I get anxious when I think
  (anticipate) a certain outcome because I work hard and I
  deserve it. I tend to think about (ruminate) my past and
  worry about my future because I am alone. I am old.
  I feel much better physically and mentally compared to
  what I felt last year, but I still have a void that I
  want to share my life with someone, where I can rest

my wings safely and I would like to do so to this person. Anything external things are out of my control. Whether I get external validation or not is something I don't have any control over it. I am responsible to validate myself good or bad and it doesn't matter what the outcome's going to be. All I can do is to have an attitude to learn from it whether the outcome is good or bad. And apply the learnings to the next challenge. This is kind of exciting, isn't it !

- The outcome of my last relationship was very bad. From it, I learned who I am ~ and how I want to live my life my values and my philosophy. I would like to be with some one who understand and appreciate that. This means some one who is mature and educated.

- In Any situation and any ~~real~~ relationship, as I wrote it in my diary today, all I can do is to try to do my best in every moment. My attitude toward the event is the most important thing in my life rather than the event itself.

11/18/23   12:25 PM

DAY 2: SEEKING TRUTH

If anyone is able to convince me and show me that I do not think or act right, I will gladly change; for I seek the truth by which no one was ever injured. But they are injured who abide in their error and ignorance.

とじまる
残る

Marcus Aurelius, *Meditations*, 6.21

Marcus Aurelius reminds us to value the truth enough to change our minds—and our behavior—when necessary. Sometimes that truth hurts, and never more so than when we are learning about ourselves. But ultimately, that discomfort allows us to grow and flourish. For Stoics, when we examine ourselves and our world as objectively as possible, we develop wisdom, understanding, and self-confidence.

1. Is the truth important to you? Why or why not? Would you rather be happy but deceived, or would you rather learn a difficult truth?
2. Do you think your ego might be tied to "being right"? What if you could let go of your need to always be right? How might you be free to explore new ideas, make a few mistakes, learn from them, and move on?

Love truth!! I don't want to be happy but deceived any more!
I would rather lean from it even it sometimes hurts!
All I can do is doing my best at every moment. Accept the
outcome whether it is good or bad because I can always
learn from it, and apply my learning to the next moment
or the next event. I am fluid and flexible. It has been
discomfort and hurting (it's still so), but this experience

of looking inner self and learning about myself and world around me is definitely allowing me to grow and flourish. I would like to keep growing and flourishing!

11/20/23   10:34 PM

DAY 3: FINDING QUIET COURAGE

> If people knew what bravery was, they would have no
> doubt as to what a brave person's conduct should be. For
> bravery is not thoughtless rashness, or love of danger, or
> the courting of fear-inspiring objects; it is the knowledge
> which enables us to distinguish between that which is evil
> and that which is not.

Seneca, *Moral Letters to Lucilius*, 85.28

Stoics remind us that courage is much more expansive than the adrenaline rush that comes with physical bravery. Seneca defines courage as doing what's right, even when it's hard. When you face your fears, stand up for what you believe, or turn your gaze inward to confront your own misgivings, you act with courage. Sometimes the quietest acts are the most courageous.

1. Write about a time when you showed quiet courage. What inspired your bravery in this situation?
2. In what ways can courage help you look inside yourself? What do you need courage to face right now?

After the years of Eric's treating me disrespectfully,
I finally stood up for myself to set a boundary and asked
him to take an accountability like what an adult man
would do. He obiously gaslighted me and confused me.
I was brave and proud of myself even I stumbled a lot
way out the door, and it took a little while to completely
seal the door.

I am still facing my fear for future, standing up for what I believe, turning my gaze inward to confront my own misgivings (this is kinda of past...). Every day and every moment, I feel like I am ~~excess~~ exercising the quiet courage. I need courage to stay away from people who disturb my serenity. I need courage ~~to have~~ not to have hopeless hope. I need courage not to lose myself.

11/21/2023   11:08 PM

DAY 4: YOUR ESSENTIAL NATURE

And what is our nature? To act as free people, as noble,
as self-respecting.

Epictetus, *Discourses*, 3.7, 26

Epictetus puts it plainly and simply: everyone—including you—is worthy of dignity and respect. Humans are curious, caring, rational, and
social. They are also messy, complex, and full of potential. Here, we
look at the relationship between inner freedom and self-respect—the
core of who you are.

1. What impedes your self-respect? List five ways you can be kinder
    to yourself. How might this kindness radiate outward?
2. Beneath self-judgment is your essential nature. What does that
    person think about? How do they carry and nourish themselves?
    Identify two ways you can start to be your essential self at home,
    at work, or in your relationships.

Feeling of lonely. Because of me not want to be lonely, I attach
to people by lowing myself = disrespecting myself. If I have
to disrespect myself to attatch certain types of people, it is
not right for me. Respecting myself is knowing who are
right people or not... I cannot attatch myself to an image of
I have of a person. I have to be strong enough to choose
being alone over people without good characters. I have to
respect myself enough to choose being alone over people without
good characters.

11/25/2023   12:41 PM
@ Cole's Coffee

staying away from people and situations that disturb my serenity and don't agree with my values. Creating my environment with important people and things and respect my freedom, Humility with self-respect. There is an opportunity to learn in every moment. Use things learned to make a reasoned judgement/choice. First feeling/reaction is just an impression. Take time to see each event objectively and make a reasoned judgement/choice, which let me to gain inner freedom and self-respect.   11/26/2023   12:17 AM

DAY 5: YOUR INTERNAL COMPASS

> We must set before our eyes the goal of the Supreme Good,
> towards which we may strive, and to which all our acts
> and words may have reference—just as sailors must guide
> their course according to a certain star. Life without ideals
> is erratic.
>
> Seneca, *Moral Letters to Lucilius*, 95.45–46

Seneca tells us to think carefully about our goals in life, instead of cruising through life directionless or on autopilot. Where do you want to go, and why? When you know where you're headed, every step of the journey becomes more meaningful.

1. It's 10 years in the future and you're looking back. List three aspirations your future self would be proud of.
2. Develop three concrete, big-picture goals that match up to these aspirations. What routines and habits can you develop to help you reach these goals and aspirations? List two things you can do this week to support each concrete goal.

DAY 6: FILTERING THE NONESSENTIAL

> Do what is necessary, and whatever the reason of the
> animal which is naturally social requires, and as it
> requires. For this brings not only the tranquility which
> comes from doing well, but also that which comes from
> doing few things.

> **Marcus Aurelius, *Meditations*, 4.24**

Marcus Aurelius reminds us to think carefully and critically about what matters. The goal is to develop the habit of asking yourself, "Is this really necessary?" This applies to decisions about where to go, what to do, and whom to spend time with. When you filter out unnecessary distractions, you leave room for reflection, meaning, and fulfillment.

1. Make a list of tasks and activities you perform on an average day. Review the list and think carefully about how important or meaningful each activity is. Can you eliminate any from your life? If so, cross them off. Which uplifting project or big-picture goal will you replace it with?

2. How can you ensure that nonmeaningful activities don't make their way back into your schedule? What mental filters can you use? Develop a mantra—a simple phrase—you can repeat to remind yourself to cut mindless or harmful habits.

DAY 7: RESPECTING YOUR ESSENCE

> Since, then, it is inevitable that every person, whoever they be, should deal with each thing according to the opinion which they form about it, these few who think that by their birth they are called to fidelity, to self-respect, and to unerring judgment in the use of external impressions, cherish no mean or ignoble thoughts about themselves, whereas the multitude do quite the opposite.

Epictetus, *Discourses*, 1.3, 4

When we find an opportunity for progress, do we choose to take the leap or hold ourselves back? Epictetus says that our beliefs about ourselves play a key role in our choices. If we decide to align ourselves with excellence, courage, and self-respect, we will rise to (almost) every occasion.

1. Do you ever have unkind or overly critical thoughts about yourself? Write them down here.
2. What if you learned those unkind thoughts are not objectively true? What would happen if you substituted different and more helpful thoughts? Rewrite each disparaging thought from a new, more supportive angle. Identify one choice you can make today to shift from damaging to self-respecting beliefs about yourself.

DAY 8: A SECOND LOOK AT JUDGMENT

Consider that everything is opinion, and opinion is in your power. Take away then, when you choose, your opinion, and like a mariner, who has doubled the promontory, you will find calm, everything stable, and a waveless bay.

Marcus Aurelius, *Meditations*, **12.22**

Snap judgments about situations, people, or ourselves are not objective truths. They are opinions, stories we tell about a situation and our projection on it. Sometimes these stories help us make sense of the world, but sometimes they make things worse. Marcus Aurelius reminds us that by curbing our negative judgments, we escape the turbulence of our emotions.

1. Choose a scenario where you've made snap judgments: (a) meeting someone new; (b) entering a job interview; (c) having an argument with a friend or partner. Go back and carefully examine each judgment. Are they factually true, or are they opinions? Could anything else be true?

2. How would questioning your judgments allow you to feel calmer and interact more effectively? Write down one judgment to release. Sit with that writing for 30 seconds. How do you feel now?

DAY 9: BETWEEN STIMULUS AND RESPONSE

If you are pained by any external thing, it is not this thing that disturbs you, but your own judgment about it. And it is in your power to wipe out this judgment now. But if anything in your own disposition gives you pain, who hinders you from correcting your opinion?

Marcus Aurelius, *Meditations*, 8.47

Marcus Aurelius asks, "Who hinders you from correcting your opinion?" (Hint: it's you.) When we carefully examine our negative emotions, we see a gap between a negative stimulus (what happened) and our emotional response (how we feel about it). He reminds us that power comes from removing judgment around an external stimulus and realizing that stimulus doesn't control our thoughts—we do.

1. Identify the last negative emotion you experienced. What was the stimulus? What was your judgment about the situation? When did you start to feel upset? Now pry open the gap between the negative stimulus and your emotional response. Was there space for you to change your judgment that something "bad" was happening?

2. You wake up in a bad mood. Explore a different thought pattern that's more expansive or forgiving. How does this thought pattern influence your actions?

DAY 10: BEFRIENDING YOURSELF

What pleased me today in the writings of Hecato is these words: "What progress, you ask, have I made? I have begun to be a friend to myself." That was indeed a great benefit; such a person can never be alone. You may be sure that such a person is a friend to all humankind.

Seneca, *Moral Letters to Lucilius*, 6.7

Seneca reminds us that being a true friend to yourself is the first step in becoming a true friend to others. When you are deeply confident in yourself, you rely less on external validation and, in so doing, create room to accept others as they are. We can have high standards and still show ourselves compassion when we, or others, struggle to meet them.

1. Do you treat yourself as well as you treat your friends? Stand in front of a mirror and name five qualities about yourself that you take pride in.

2. Identify one area where you tend to be critical of yourself. Write a message to yourself—as you would write to a friend—showing compassion and encouragement.

DAY 11: TIGHTENING VALUES

If it is not right, do not do it: if it is not true, do not say it.

Marcus Aurelius, *Meditations,* **12.17**

Marcus Aurelius gets to the heart of the relationship between values and action. If we value internal goods like intentionality and acceptance, our impulses and actions will reflect these ideals. Living in alignment with your values does not mean being perfect or eliminating desire from your life. It's about tightening the connection between your values and your impulses so that your actions reflect your desire for good.

1. Instead of trying to suppress your impulses, think in terms of redirecting them toward goals you deem noble. What goals are worthy of your energy? What values do they signal? Now identify three or four impulses that can support these goals.

2. Whenever you feel internal conflict, what can you tell yourself to get back on track? Write a short mantra you can memorize to repeat when you find yourself compromising your values.

DAY 12: CALMING YOUR NERVOUS SYSTEM

The primary indication, to my thinking, of a well-ordered mind is a person's ability to remain in one place and linger in their own company.

Seneca, *Moral Letters to Lucilius*, 2.1

The constant stream of news, entertainment, work, and social media puts our nervous systems into hyperdrive. Our brains are chronically alert, responding to short-term threats and rewards. It's no wonder we can't relax. Seneca teaches us to find peace by disconnecting and spending time with ourselves. When you slow down and get to know yourself, you become deeply aware of your own sensations and thoughts. You begin to truly appreciate your experience of the world.

1. Silence all your devices and put them in a different room. Set a timer for 15 minutes and sit with yourself. What do you notice about yourself when there are no devices near you? What does your mind do? What does this experience feel like?

2. If you spent 15 minutes every day just enjoying your own company, what do you think you would learn about yourself?

_____

_____

_____

_____

_____

_____

_____

_____

_____

_____

_____

_____

_____

_____

_____

_____

_____

_____

_____

_____

_____

_____

_____

_____

_____

_____

_____

_____

DAY 13: WRESTLING WITH RESTLESSNESS

> The person you are matters more than the place to which you go . . . As it is, however, you are not journeying; you are drifting and being driven, only exchanging one place for another, although that which you seek—to live well—is found everywhere.
>
> Seneca, *Moral Letters to Lucilius*, 28.4–5

Seneca tells us the secret to a calm and content mind is finding happiness in who you are and where you are right now. It's easy to become overexcited by new people, places, and things. Who doesn't love the thrill of new adventures? But if we're not satisfied with what we have today, we run the risk of always striving—in other words, never finding fulfillment.

1. Take a closer look at what meets your needs by writing down five things you appreciate in your life right now. This could be as simple as the cup of coffee you enjoy in the morning.
2. Do you agree with Seneca's idea that you should change your mind, not your location, if you want to live well? Why or why not?

DAY 14: A CLOSER LOOK AT YOUR GIFTS

But for determining the rational and the irrational, we employ not only our estimates of the value of external things, but also the criterion of that which is in keeping with one's own character.

Epictetus, *Discourses*, 1.2, 7

Each of us has our own personality, life experiences, and circumstances. That means we all have different desires and needs. For Epictetus, knowing your aptitudes, preferences, and disposition helps you stay true to yourself—and breeds compassion for others along the way.

1. What is your greatest gift? What do you offer the world? It can be big or small. Be honest with yourself. If nothing comes to mind, consider calling a family member or mentor for a supportive perspective.

2. What does self-knowledge have to do with passion? Consider one thing you know to be absolutely true about yourself. How has this truth informed what you want in life?

DAY 15: HAVE YOU MET ME?

Someone who meets a person as a person is one who learns to understand the other's judgments, and in their turn exhibits their own. Learn to know my judgments; show me your own, and then say you have met me.

Epictetus, *Discourses*, 3.9, 12–13

Rather than looking at someone's wealth, career success, or social status, look closely at their values and choices. How do they treat other people? How do they react to frustration? Observing their choices allows you to know them at a deeper level—and reflect on your own patterns.

1. Think about someone you like and respect. Peel back their outermost layers (appearance, age, profession, etc.) and think about their character. What does this person value in life? What aspects of their character draw you to them? What does your gravitation toward them say about you?

2. Do you surround yourself with people of good character? What clues do you look for? What types of behavior are you drawn to and why?

DAY 16: FROM FOE TO FRIEND

When another blames you or hates you, or when people say about you anything injurious, approach their poor souls, penetrate within, and see what kind of people they are. You will discover that there is no reason to take any trouble that these people may have this or that opinion about you. However you must be well disposed towards them, for by nature they are friends.

Marcus Aurelius, *Meditations*, 9.27

Marcus Aurelius reminds us that when we remove our dependence on someone else's opinion, we create enough space to see their humanity. By observing their opinions without attaching ourselves to them (when we don't take their words personally), we put down the burden of someone else's judgment. We disempower their negativity and, at our best, leave room to understand them—perhaps enough to make a friend.

1. Think about the last time you were stung by someone's disapproval or rejection. Why did you want their approval? As best you can, reflect on the person's character, motivation, and judgments. Given this new perspective, could you break free from their judgment?
2. Write a dialogue between two people who have a misunderstanding. Craft one version where the disagreement escalates. Write another where it deescalates. Record what you observe about the differences in word choice and (imagined) tone.

DAY 17: YOUR INNER CITADEL

Pay attention to your sense-impressions, and watch over
them sleeplessly. For it is no small matter that you are
guarding, but self-respect, and fidelity, and constancy,
a state of mind undisturbed by passion, pain, fear, or
confusion—in a word, freedom. What are the things for
which you are about to sell *these* things? Look, how valuable
are they?

Epictetus, *Discourses*, 4.3, 7–8

The Stoics considered the mind to be a sanctuary—your inner citadel,
as they called it. When guided by Stoicism, we see how intimately self-
respect is tied to attention: if we do not pay attention to what we allow
into our minds, we do not protect ourselves from harmful thoughts.
What thoughts do you allow to live in your head? This question is the
key to developing self-respect and inner freedom.

1. Set a timer for two minutes and examine what enters your mind.
   Then, write down one or two of the thoughts you observed. Seeing
   these thoughts on the page may help you view them objectively.
2. What lies in your inner citadel? Or better yet, what type of
   thoughts do you allow into and out of this mental sanctuary?

DAY 18: THE SAME STANDARD OF FORGIVENESS

It is not fit that I should give myself pain, for I have never intentionally given pain even to another.

Marcus Aurelius, *Meditations*, 8.42

Marcus Aurelius reminds us how important it is to prioritize self-compassion. If we wouldn't say something harmful to someone else, why is it okay to say it to ourselves? For Stoics, fairness allows room for forgiveness and patience for ourselves as much as for others.

1. There's a difference between having high ethical standards and being hard on yourself: with the former, you recognize room for improvement (healing), and with the latter, you cause undue self-criticism (hurting). Go back to Day 10 and read the compassionate things you wrote about yourself. Have you shown yourself more kindness this week? If not, what's stopping you?

2. Write down any harsh thoughts you are having about yourself right now. Examine them carefully. Can you tend to any of these wounds right now?

DAY 19: GOODBYE, EXTERNAL VALIDATION

> How do I any longer hold correct judgments when I am not
> satisfied with being the person that I am, but am excited
> about what other people will think of me?

> Epictetus, *Discourses*, 4.6, 24

For Stoics, it's impossible to view the world rationally when we are
tied up in others' opinions of us. That means releasing our attachment
to others' criticism *and* praise. Our character and happiness don't
depend on other people's opinions—good or bad—so why give them
power? Staying focused on inner success means letting go of approval
and disapproval from those we admire, love, and fear.

1. What would happen if the person you admire most in this world
    disapproved of you? Would it fundamentally change your desires
    and goals? Would you be a better or worse person after receiving
    their judgment?
2. Write down five nice things you want to hear about yourself. Write
    them down or say them in the mirror for as long as it takes to stop
    wishing they came from someone else.

DAY 20: A HUMBLE STOREFRONT

> Do the one thing that can render you really happy: cast
> aside and trample under foot those things that glitter
> outwardly . . . look toward the true good, and rejoice only
> in that which comes from your own store. And what do I
> mean by "from your own store"? I mean from your very
> self, that which is the best part of you.
>
> Seneca, *Moral Letters to Lucilius*, 23.6

It's hard not to want to strive for accolades—for money, fame, power,
or prestige—or the comfort of having the things we want when we
want them. But Stoic wisdom tells us that wisdom, justice, courage,
and temperance are always available at our own store. In fact, there's
an endless supply. For Stoics, the real work comes from locating and
cashing in acceptance, approval, and self-worth. No credit card—or
external validation—necessary.

1. What accolades have you strived for in your life? Did you feel
    fundamentally different or better after you received them? Do the
    same thing for big purchases you convinced yourself would bring
    you happiness.
2. Write down the emotional "goods" you've gathered from others
    by identifying specific phrases you've wanted to hear. Can you tie
    them to emotions? Was there ever a deficit of these emotions in
    your life?

DAY 21: STAYING ON THE PATH

Be not disgusted, nor discouraged, nor dissatisfied, if
you do not succeed in doing everything according to
right principles; but when you have failed, return back
again, and be content if the greater part of what you do
is consistent with human nature, and love this to which
you return.

Marcus Aurelius, *Meditations*, 5.9

The Stoics never said inner excellence was easy. If you have chosen
to pursue a path of virtue—greatness of spirit, elevation of mind, and
a more intentional life—you are aiming for the highest potential of
human nature. As Marcus Aurelius reminds us, it's a lifelong project,
and we can't lose heart if the road is long and winding. We may sometimes fall short of our lofty goals, but we are better people for having
tried. In other words: it's human to make mistakes; the important
thing is to stay on the path.

1. Write down the single most important goal to you right now. Can
    you come up with a name for this path? Now imagine this path
    is a tree trunk with branches taking you from its center. What
    branches are steering you away from your goal? Write them down.
    (It helps to sketch this out.)
2. Write about the last time you showed moral weakness. What did
    you learn from this event? Was there anything positive to gain
    from this so-called failure?

DAY 22: FINDING YOUR GENIUS

You must decide whether your disposition is better suited for vigorous action or for tranquil speculation and contemplation, and you must adopt whichever the bent of your genius inclines you for.

Seneca, *Of Peace of Mind*, 7.2

The Stoics urge us to work with our talents, not against them. They recognized that we are by nature better suited for some roles than others. While a growth mindset is a valuable tool ("I can't do that *yet*"), it's also true that humans display vastly different kinds of "genius." Of course there are times when we must study a subject, take a job, or perform a duty that goes against our natural inclinations. But when given a choice, Stoics urge us to align our energy with our aptitude.

1. On Day 14 you wrote about your character, personality, and gifts. Drawing on your self-knowledge, identify one or two ways you can incorporate your talents into your life right now. How can you find fulfillment through your natural gifts?
2. If you're thinking about making a career change or a major life decision, which of your talents and preferences will impact that decision? How can you incorporate your natural gifts into a life of fulfillment and excellence?

DAY 23: LIGHTING YOUR INNER FLAME

Just as the flame springs straight into the air and cannot be cabined or kept down any more than it can repose in quiet, so our soul is always in motion, and the more ardent it is, the greater its motion and activity. But happy is the [person] who has given it this impulse toward better things!

Seneca, *Moral Letters to Lucilius*, 39.3

What inspires you? Great music, books, and conversations with friends? Spend some time thinking about what lights your inner flame and keeps your spirit burning brightly. Identify the activities that bring you joy and meaning and find ways to incorporate them into your life more. Rekindle your inner fire by directing your energy toward those things that bring you unbridled joy.

1. Think back to the times you've felt most alive, most in tune with yourself and your environment. What were you doing? Identify at least three activities that kindle your inner flame. How can you fit more of them into your current life?

2. Write a letter to your childhood hero. (You won't actually send this letter.) Tell them about what has brought you the most joy in each decade of your life. Don't think too hard about the answers. Write the first things that come to mind. Reread the letter. Do you see any common threads?

DAY 24: SWAPPING PITY FOR PRODUCTIVENESS

What shall perturb me, or trouble me, or seem grievous
to me? Shall I fail to use my faculty to that end for which
I have received it, but grieve and lament over things that
occur?—"Yes, but my nose is running."—What have you
hands for, then? Is it not that you may wipe your nose? . . .
How much better it would be for you to wipe your nose
than to find fault!

Epictetus, *Discourses*, 1.6, 28–32

We are all tempted toward self-pity sometimes. But everyone has
hardship in their life, and self-pity never helps anything. Stoics
believe that rather than lamenting our situation, it's more productive
to consider the resources and tools we have available to solve the
problem. What does it look like to creatively tackle an issue? What
does it feel like to replace pity with productiveness and appreciation?

1. In the past three days, have you experienced self-pity? Describe
    what triggered it. Can you tie it to a specific habit or circum-
    stance? Write down the resources you have (including people,
    knowledge, and skills) to deal with what caused the pity.
2. Describe a hardship you face. Name five things relating to the
    hardship that are out of your control. Now name five things that
    are within your control. Record how it feels to identify that which
    you can and cannot control. Which will you give more energy to?

DAY 25: YOUR INTERNAL APPLAUSE

When I see a person in anxiety, I say to myself, What can it be that this person wants? For if they did not want something that was outside of their control, how could they still remain in anxiety? That is why the cithara player when singing all alone shows no anxiety, but does so when he enters the theater, even though he has a very beautiful voice and plays the cithara admirably; for he does not wish merely to sing well, but also to win applause, and that is no longer under his control.

Epictetus, *Discourses*, 2.13, 1–2

The impulse to win others' affection can lead to intense desire, even anxiety. When we become invested in other people's opinions about our work, actions, or persona, we relinquish our power. We also strip much of the joy out of the action, focusing on the performance above the act itself. For Stoics, the only applause that matters is that which we quietly give ourselves.

1. Think of a time when you needed another person's approval. What was the scenario? Why did you want their praise? Write a short note to yourself in that moment giving yourself the validation you craved. The key: write this note in your voice, not anyone else's.
2. List three things you would like to learn or try but have held yourself back from for fear of failure or imperfection. Visualize yourself doing these things poorly but having an incredible time as you do. When you remove the performance aspect of these activities, do you desire them more or less?

DAY 26: THE ANXIETY ANTIDOTE

Let not future things disturb you, for you will come to them, if it shall be necessary, having with you the same reason which now you use for present things.

Marcus Aurelius, *Meditations*, 7.8

Our minds sometimes fall into the worry trap, ping-ponging through possible future scenarios. For Stoics, the way to minimize anxiety about the future is twofold: (a) stay grounded in the present, and (b) trust that your inner resources—your mind and character—will be sufficient to deal with future difficulties. Marcus Aurelius reminds us that while we cannot control the future, we can apply our attributes to the predictable and unforeseen. One antidote to anxiety is to trust in ourselves.

1. Look around you. List three stationary things you see in your immediate vicinity. Focus on these objects. What do they tell you about where you are? How do you feel when you recognize your own stillness?
2. What inner resources do you possess to deal with hardship? Write about how you have used these characteristics to deal with challenges in the past.

DAY 27: KEEPING THINGS SIMPLE

> Think of those things only about which if one should
> suddenly ask, What have you now in your thoughts? With
> perfect openness you might immediately answer, This
> or That; so that from your words it should be plain that
> everything in you is simple and benevolent.

> Marcus Aurelius, *Meditations*, 3.4

Marcus Aurelius describes an inner simplicity that keeps only the thoughts that enrich and enhance your character, while clearing away unhealthy mental clutter. If you notice a thought or mental habit that holds you back from excellence and growth, toss it out. Pruning away values and mental habits that don't contribute to your long-term flourishing is a Stoic secret to inner tranquility.

1. What does "inner simplicity" mean to you? Describe your mindset when you are most at peace. What are you thinking or not thinking about? Where are you physically? Write down one way you can put more energy into cultivating this simple and benevolent state of mind.

2. Identify three or four themes your mind returns to when it's wandering. Are you worried? Angry? Anxious about not being good enough? For each theme you identified, write an encouraging response ready to combat it.

DAY 28: STICKING TO YOUR STORY

You know what I mean by a good person? One who is complete, finished—whom no constraint or need can render bad. I see such a person in you, if only you go steadily on and bend to your task, and see to it that all your actions and words harmonize and correspond with each other and are stamped in the same mold. If a person's acts are out of harmony, their soul is crooked.

Seneca, *Moral Letters to Lucilius*, 34.3–4

Seneca reminds us that to live a Stoic life means to align our actions with our values and principles and to live by our virtues. By consistently directing our thoughts and actions toward goals that align with our virtues, we create an internal harmony that is deeply enriching for ourselves and those around us.

1. Go back to Day 5 and review your big-picture life goals. In the past day, did your thoughts and actions reflect these goals? Write down specific examples of actions that helped or hindered you on your path.
2. Choose one or two goals to work on. Explain how you will work toward your goal this week, this month, and for the rest of the year.

DAY 29: IT'S YOUR LIFE TO LIVE

Now nothing gets us into greater troubles than our subservience to common rumor, and our habit of thinking that those things are best which are most generally received as such, of taking many counterfeits for truly good things, and of living not by reason but by imitation of others.

Seneca, *Of a Happy Life*, 1.3

Seneca reminds us that to be subservient to public opinion, without the due diligence of self-reflection and analysis, is to live a counterfeit life. To live a rich internal life, we must arrive at our own conclusions, remain curious students of this one precious life, and make the quest for understanding a daily ritual.

1. Choose one of your deeply held values to examine closely. How did you acquire it? Were you nudged toward this value by people or events around you? Does your culture encourage or discourage this value? Does this value align with your vision of who you want to be right now?

2. List one thing you have always wanted to do but haven't for fear of what others might think. If you feel yourself struggling, write down the first thing that comes to mind. What is one action you can take today to live more boldly, in alignment with your true passions and free from fear of judgment? After all, it's your life to live.

DAY 30: TIME FOR YOUR FIG

Nothing great comes into being all at once; why, not even does the bunch of grapes, or a fig. If you say to me now, "I want a fig," I shall answer, "That requires time." Let the tree blossom first, then put forth its fruit, and finally let the fruit ripen. Now although the fruit of even a fig-tree is not brought to perfection all at once and in a single hour, would you still seek to secure the fruit of a person's mind in so short a while and so easily?

Epictetus, *Discourses*, 1.15, 7–8

We all want immediate results. But as Epictetus states here, it's important to be patient with yourself as you undertake this difficult but meaningful journey. Keep returning to your practice, returning to your sources, and returning to your*self*. Despite droughts and other unforeseen obstacles, the result will be an abundance of figs.

1. Look at your journal entry from Day 1. Have you seen any growth or progress in the three areas you identified for change? Record anything different you notice about yourself.
2. List one time you had to exercise tremendous patience. Was it worth it? How did you regulate your excitement? Write down three things that ground you when you feel restless or impatient.

THE
ROAD TO
ACCEPTANCE

In the first 30 days, you made progress toward living with greater self-compassion, finding strength in your inner resources, and relying on your own internal applause. In Course B, you'll deepen your acceptance and find peace with those around you. You'll discover mental tools and techniques to approach life's challenges with wisdom, cultivating gratitude for the present moment. Key targets in the next 30 days are becoming more proactive, resilient, and ready to engage with the world.

DAY 31: NO TIME LIKE RIGHT NOW

Postponement is the greatest waste of life; it deprives people of each day as it comes, it snatches from them the present by promising something hereafter. The greatest hindrance to living is expectancy, which depends upon the morrow and wastes today ... At what goal do you aim? All things that are still to come lie in uncertainty; live straightway!

Seneca, *On the Shortness of Life*, 9.1

What is the greatest threat to the present? Putting things off until tomorrow—or worse, expecting things will be magically better tomorrow. Seneca reminds us that there is no time like right now to tackle that which we want to confront or achieve. While time is uncertain, our action—in the present moment—is something we can count on.

1. Describe a day in your life when you are fully present for each moment. Detail your inner experience, including your mindset and emotions.
2. What opportunities are open to you in the present? Identify one you will seize today.

DAY 32: CHANGING YOUR MIND

Today I have got out of all trouble, or rather I have cast
out all trouble, for it was not outside, but within and in
my opinions.

Marcus Aurelius, *Meditations*, 9.13

Marcus Aurelius teaches us that when you change your opinions, you
change your whole mind. Using that knowledge, we can change our
opinions about things that happen to us in life. People or situations
that used to seem upsetting can become neutral or maybe even positive. The object didn't change—your perspective did.

1. Write about a time when you changed your mind about a person,
   object, or situation. Did the object change, or did you learn to see
   it in a new light?
2. Identify something or someone in your life that you strongly dis-
   like. Is it possible that you could change your opinion about it or
   them? How would your life be different if you learned to like (or at
   least feel neutral) about this person or thing?

DAY 33: TO REACT OR NOT TO REACT?

Some things are under our control, while others are not under our control. Under our control are opinion, choice, desire, aversion, and in a word, everything that is our own doing.

Epictetus, *Handbook*, 1.1

Epictetus reminds us that while we may not control what happens around us, we do have control over our opinions, choices, and actions about and in response to external stimuli. Sometimes the only things we can do are try to create space between ourselves and the situation, and adapt our attitude around it. That isn't to say we are powerless; in fact, it's the opposite. To recognize what we can control is the ultimate form of liberation.

1. Identify the last time you felt annoyed. What was the root cause of your feelings? What factors were outside of your control? Now look at that situation from a different angle. What *could* you control? What was up to you in the situation?
2. Write about a time when you had an extreme emotional response—an internal or external response—to someone. Did you hold it in or express your rage? Write down what an immediate reaction and a thoughtful reaction would have looked like. Which one feels more aligned with your values?

DAY 34: CURBING THE CONSUMPTION CRAVING

To have whatsoever they wish is in no one's power; it is in their power not to wish for what they have not, but cheerfully to employ what comes.

Seneca, *Moral Letters to Lucilius*, 123.3

We can all think of things we'd like to have more of. The problem is, once we start pinning our happiness on getting more of something, we're never satisfied with what we have. Once our wishes are fulfilled, we move on to wanting the next thing in an endless (and expensive) cycle of consumption. For Seneca, a wiser (and more cost-effective) strategy is to learn to be happy with what we already have. That includes tangible and intangible goods, like your generosity and kind spirit.

1. Write a list of 10 intangible things you are grateful for. Add 10 more things that you can see or touch with your hands. (Notice: does focusing on these items make you feel gratitude or inspire you to want more?)
2. Write down three things to celebrate in your life right now. Explain why you appreciate them.

DAY 35: DEALING WITH IMPERFECT HUMANS

When you are offended with any person's shameless conduct, immediately ask yourself, Is it possible, then, that shameless people should not be in the world? It is not possible. Do not, then, require what is impossible.

Marcus Aurelius, *Meditations*, **9.42**

Dealing with less-than-optimal people and situations is an unavoidable part of life. For Stoics, the key is to focus less on the external (the person) and more on the internal (our response to the person). Marcus Aurelius reminds us our response is in our control (i.e., it's possible for the annoying to become more tolerable). Part of shaping our future actions involves understanding our relationship to our triggers and responses.

1. Recall someone who has rubbed you the wrong way. What triggers your negative emotion? List three specific actions or behaviors.
2. Write out three possible responses to each trigger: one negative, one neutral, and one very positive. (It may be difficult, but with some imagination you *can* think of a positive response to a difficult person.) Challenge: select one of these responses to use the next time you encounter this trigger. Why do you think this response will be beneficial?

DAY 36: RESPECT IN DISAGREEMENT

Humans exist for the sake of one another. Teach them then or bear with them.

Marcus Aurelius, *Meditations*, 8.59

It can be challenging to deal with someone who doesn't share your values in life. But the Stoics believed every person is worthy of respect, even if you perceive them to be morally misguided. Our job is not to get angry with them but to be a role model. Stoic wisdom urges us to keep these two points in mind: First, no one makes mistakes willingly—they think they are doing the right thing. Second, you can still find contentment, no matter what other people do. In other words, we can respond constructively, encouraging them to rethink their actions, while still showing them respect.

1. Think of someone you're struggling to get along with. How might that person believe they are doing the right thing? Describe the situation *from the other person's point of view*. In this situation, will you teach them or bear with them? Explain how you will do this.
2. Does another person's character have any impact on your character? Why or why not?

DAY 37: THE ART OF PREPAREDNESS

Everyone approaches courageously a danger which
they have prepared themselves to meet long before,
and withstands even hardships if they have previously
practiced how to meet them. But, contrariwise, the
unprepared are panic-stricken even at the most trifling
things. We must see to it that nothing shall come upon
us unforeseen.

Seneca, *Moral Letters to Lucilius*, 107.4

For Seneca, one of the most important ways to deal with hardship is
to prepare for it. But how do we do this? The "premeditation of adversity" is an ancient technique that helps us prepare for challenges. You
visualize the very outcome that you fear most, then envision how you
would deal with this outcome. If the event does come to pass, you'll
have an action plan ready. And if it never happens, you can be grateful and move on.

1. Identify a challenge you're facing today. What is your top concern
    about this challenge? Imagine this concern comes true. How will
    you respond? Be detailed and specific about your response. What
    will you think, say, and do?
2. Does being prepared allow you to be more courageous in the
    moment? Write about the relationship, if any, between prepared-
    ness and courage.

DAY 38: BUILDING GOOD HABITS

> If you want to do something, make a habit of it; if you want not to do something, refrain from doing it, and accustom yourself to something else instead. The same principle holds true in the affairs of the mind also; when you are angry, you may be sure, not merely that this evil has befallen you, but also that you have strengthened the habit and have, as it were, added fuel to the flame.

> Epictetus, *Discourses*, 2.18, 4–5

The ancient Stoics understood the power of habit. If you allow your mind to ruminate on the negative (for example, you don't want to go to work), you are creating a mental habit (in this instance, of dissatisfaction). Will you turn your thoughts toward wisdom and excellence or misjudgment and dissatisfaction?

1. Identify a mental habit you would like to change. What are some triggers that often set off your bad habit?
2. When you feel a bad habit coming on, what could you think about instead? Select a mantra, a virtue, or a positive goal (like tranquility or happiness) to focus on. Consider keeping a log to record your progress over the next week.

DAY 39: USING YOUR RESOURCES

Call good sense to your aid against difficulties: it is possible to soften what is harsh, to widen what is too narrow, and to make heavy burdens press less severely upon one who bears them skillfully.

Seneca, *Of Peace of Mind*, 10.4

Stoics urge us to examine our resources, skills, experience, mindset, and strength of character as we confront adversity. Even though we can't change the nature of the world, we can learn to shift our vantage point and cope with it effectively. When a difficult situation arises, will you allow anger and frustration to cloud your mind? Or will you be able to remember that difficulties are a normal part of life?

1. Identify one difficulty you are dealing with right now. What is it within your power to change about this situation? What is it not within your power to change? List five internal and five external resources you possess to skillfully cope with this challenge.
2. Take Seneca's phrase and list one way to "soften what is harsh," one way to "widen what is too narrow," and one way to "make heavy burdens press less severely," as they apply to your life.

DAY 40: ACCEPTING CONSTANT CHANGE

The unripe grape, the ripe bunch, the dried grape, all are changes, not into nothing, but into something which exists not yet.

Marcus Aurelius, *Meditations*, 11.35

Change is simply a passage from one state to another. Stoics urge us to embrace change as a natural part of life, rather than fighting it. When we learn to experience change not as a breakdown but as a transition to something new, we can peacefully accept even difficult changes like aging, illness, and loss.

1. Look back over the past year. Write down at least two changes that have impacted your life. How did you react to these changes?
2. Describe a major transition you experienced in your life as the movement from one condition to another. Try to write objectively, like a scientist describing the results of an experiment.

DAY 41: LIVING IN HARSH CONDITIONS

No tree which the wind does not often blow against is firm and strong; for it is stiffened by the very act of being shaken, and plants its roots more securely: those which grow in a sheltered valley are brittle.

Seneca, *Of Providence*, 4.16

Seneca reminds us that although difficult conditions might not be ideal, they are a lever for learning new skills, building confidence, and learning to trust ourselves. As with trees, harsh conditions strengthen the human spirit, helping us develop grit and resilience. When we change our perspective on adversity, our life changes too.

1. Identify one major challenge you have dealt with in your life. What was the worst part about it? Now shift your perspective. In what ways did it strengthen your character? Would you rewrite history if you could?

2. Describe yourself as a tree. Do you have strong roots and branches? What made them this way? What are they able to withstand? Are there brittle parts you would like to strengthen?

DAY 42: THE GOOD WITHIN

The principal task in life is this: distinguish matters and weigh them one against another, and say to yourself, "Externals are not under my control; moral choice is under my control. Where am I to look for the good and evil? Within me, in that which is my own."

Epictetus, *Discourses*, 2.5, 4–5

The Stoics return to it again and again: How do we let go of the external things we cannot control and instead find power in our choices? Epictetus shows us that the choices we make are rooted in our character, and our character, in turn, is shaped by our choices. How we perceive the world is largely a product of what exists within and relates to our capacity for moral growth.

1. Describe a time when you were faced with a moral decision. What were the external circumstances? What could you and couldn't you control?
2. Name one thing you admire about your perspective on the world. Is there anything you tend to think negatively about? How can you align it to the thing you admire most about your perspective?

DAY 43: INTENTION OVER OUTCOME

> The wise person regards the reason for all their actions, but not the results. The beginning is in our own power; fortune decides the issue, but I do not allow fortune to pass sentence upon myself.
>
> Seneca, *Moral Letters to Lucilius*, 14.16

Although we don't control the outcome of our actions, Seneca reminds us that we do control our input, including our intentions. Our moral choices take place at the level of our intentions—what do we want to bring to the world? Stoics aim to focus on input rather than outcome.

1. Identify a personal obstacle you'd like to overcome, writing down the intentions you plan to bring to this issue. Now draw two columns. In column A, list the factors within your control (input); in column B, list the factors outside your control (outcome). Where do your intentions belong?

2. Write about the interaction between wise discernment, or wisdom, and fate. How do they relate to one another? Is there ever tension between the two?

DAY 44: LIFE'S RHYTHMS

To have contemplated human life for forty years is the same as to have contemplated it for ten thousand years. For what more will you see?

Marcus Aurelius, *Meditations*, 7.49

Births, marriages, deaths, love, grief, joy, losses, discoveries—the details may be different, but there is a universal pattern to human life. Stoics urge us to find the beauty in these grand rhythms of life, reminding us what an honor it is to be part of this vast and magnificent cosmic story.

1. How is your life like that of a person from the past? Compare yourself to someone in your lineage or an imaginary figure from any historical period. How does expanding your mind to past generations help you better understand your life right now?

2. What aspects of life today do you think will be the same 100 years from now?

DAY 45: FACING SOLITUDE OR A CROWD

If circumstances bring you to spend your life alone or
in the company of a few, call it peace, and utilize the
condition for its proper end; converse with yourself,
exercise your sense-impressions, develop your
preconceptions. If, however, you fall in with a crowd,
call it games, a festival, a holiday, try to keep holiday
with the people.

Epictetus, *Discourses*, 4.4, 26–27

The Stoics show us that no matter where we are and who we're with,
we can learn to appreciate the state of our lives. Whether you're naturally introverted or extroverted, you can find something to love about
your circumstances and companions, whether it's a time of solitude or
you're amid a large crowd.

1. When you're alone, what activities do you find enjoyable and ben-
    eficial? How can you get to know yourself better?
2. Among small groups of friends, how can you cultivate a strong
    bond with others? How would you get to know their characters? If
    you dislike crowds, write about how you can enjoy your next gather-
    ing. Could you enjoy thinking about the shared purpose that brings
    this group together, or the individual stories within the group?

DAY 46: BEARING MISFORTUNE NOBLY

Will this which has happened prevent you from being
just, magnanimous, temperate, prudent, secure against
inconsiderate opinions and falsehood; will it prevent
you from having modesty, freedom, and everything else,
by the presence of which one's nature obtains all that is
its own? Remember too on every occasion which leads
you to vexation to apply this principle: not that this is a
misfortune, but that to bear it nobly is good fortune.

Marcus Aurelius, *Meditations*, 4.49

We all face pain, frustration, heartache, and adversity at times. Stoics
encourage us to be thankful we have what it takes to make it through
instead of cursing our luck. With training we can learn to face these
challenges with wisdom and integrity, maintaining our goodness
despite misfortune.

1. Define hardship to a 5-year-old, a 20-year-old, a 50-year-old, and
    a centenarian. What differences, if any, do you notice? What does
    this tell you about hardship and the passage of time?
2. For Marcus Aurelius, to bear misfortune nobly is to experience
    good fortune. Write about a time you experienced something ful-
    filling or fruitful in the midst of tragedy or pain.

DAY 47: WHICH HANDLE WILL YOU HOLD?

Everything has two handles, by one of which it ought to be carried and by the other not. If your brother wrongs you, do not lay hold of the matter by the handle of the wrong that he is doing . . . but rather by the other handle—that he is your brother, that you were brought up together, and then you will be laying hold of the matter by the handle by which it ought to be carried.

Epictetus, *Handbook*, 43

Epictetus reminds us of the importance of perspective and agency. (There is more than one way to look at a situation!) You choose not only how to handle a situation but also how you *perceive* the way someone should approach their responsibility. When you can discern what is just or unjust, can you nevertheless opt to find compassion—to see your connectedness—even when someone may be holding the wrong handle?

1. Identify a time in the past few days when you felt sad, frustrated, or angry with someone else and reacted negatively. Draw a pot with two handles. This will represent a time someone frustrated you in the past few days. Near the left handle, write down the other person's actions and your feelings around them. Near the right handle, write down the ways you are connected to this person and the values you share.

2. Write about a time you dropped the pot, so to speak, because you were so focused on holding the wrong handle.

DAY 48: LIVING BY EXAMPLE

> Socrates bore very firmly in mind that no one is master
> over another's governing principle . . . While they are
> attending to their own business as they think best, he
> himself none the less is in a state of harmony with nature,
> attending only to his own business, to the end that they
> also may be in harmony with nature.

> Epictetus, *Discourses*, 4.5, 4–5

Epictetus reminds us that we don't control other people. We can do
our best to influence them, but we don't control their thoughts and
behavior. When we make peace with the limits of our influence, we
can demonstrate how living in harmony with nature (that's Stoic ter-
minology for living virtuously) brings happiness.

1.   Do you agree with Epictetus that we should think in terms of pos-
     itive influence rather than control? How can you impact people
     around you as a role model?
2.   Think of a time when someone tried to force you to do something.
     How did you feel about that? How much control did they have
     over you? What lesson can you learn from that experience?

DAY 49: WHAT IF IT WERE GONE?

Think not so much of what you have not as of what you have: but of the things which you have select the best, and then reflect how eagerly they would have been sought, if you had them not.

Marcus Aurelius, *Meditations*, 7.27

We hear a lot these days about gratitude, but Marcus Aurelius offers one of the earliest and best strategies for staying grateful. Think about some of your favorite people, places, and things. Now imagine if you'd never had these things. How much would you wish to have them with you?

1. Make a list of at least 10 things you can't imagine living without— people, opportunities, and events. In an imaginary sacrifice, cross three things off the list. How does "losing" these three things change your relationship to them?

2. Name the most influential person in your life. (For the purpose of this exercise, do not include a blood relative who came before you.) Write about what your life would be like if this person had never entered it.

DAY 50: EATING SOME DIRT

The program of life is the same as that of a bathing establishment, a crowd, or a journey: sometimes things will be thrown at you, and sometimes they will strike you by accident. Life is not a dainty business.

Seneca, *Moral Letters to Lucilius*, 107.2

Seneca reminds us part of life is having mud hurled at us from time to time. Just as we shouldn't expect for life to be endlessly tragic, we also shouldn't be surprised when we experience a face full of dirt. Resilience involves wiping up the mud and keeping your sense of humor along the way.

1. Write about a time you fell flat in the mud, when you were deflated or defeated in a big way. How did you react? Would you change anything about your perspective? Was there any humor along the way?
2. Describe a time when you got caught in an unfortunate accident. What feelings came up? What inner resources did you pull from to manage the situation? What was your perspective once it was over?

DAY 51: ACCOUNTABILITY CHECK

I'm inclined to pleasure; I will betake myself to the
opposite side of the rolling ship, and that beyond measure,
so as to train myself. I am inclined to avoid hard work;
I will strain and exercise my sense-impressions to this
end, so that my aversion to everything of this kind shall
cease . . . And so different people will have to practice
particularly to meet different things.

Epictetus, *Discourses*, 3.12, 7–8

Epictetus urges us to identify aspects of our lives that need the
most improvement, then focus our efforts on those areas. Such self-
reflection can feel intrusive or downright painful, but it's essential
if we want to improve our lives. Stoics regularly ask the questions
What's my greatest weakness? How am I avoiding hard work?

1. What aspects of your character or life need improvement? Write
    down as many as you can think of. Circle the top three that have
    the biggest impact on your life.

2. Describe your process for accountability. If you don't have one,
    now is a great time to chart it out. How do you define accountabil-
    ity? How does it show up at work, in your personal life, and in the
    outside world?

The Stoic Way of Life

DAY 52: TAMING YOUR TEMPER

It is not people's acts which disturb us, for those acts have their foundation in people's ruling principles, but it is our own opinions which disturb us. Take away these opinions then, and resolve to dismiss your judgment about an act as if it were something grievous, and your anger is gone.

Marcus Aurelius, *Meditations*, 11.18

By now you know a core Stoic value is accepting that people's actions only have power when we let them. If you believe you've been wronged, you'll feel angry. When you stop believing you've been wronged, anger often dissipates. After all, isn't anger contingent upon feeling violated? While other people's behavior can certainly be offensive, unjust, or even immoral, Stoics always bear the responsibility for their reactions.

1. Do you agree with Marcus Aurelius that it's not other people's actions that disturb us but our own opinions about them? Are there any exceptions?
2. What makes it easy to get over something quickly? What makes it hard, or nearly impossible, to move through anger?

DAY 53: IN THEIR SHOES

No one considers the intention of the doer, but merely the
thing done: yet we ought to think about them, and whether
they did it intentionally or accidentally, under compulsion
or under a mistake . . . whether they did it to please
themselves or to serve a friend.

Seneca, *Of Anger*, 3.12

Stoics urge us to bring reflection to our anger. Instead of assuming
the worst, Seneca instructs us to widen our perspective about the
other person's motivation. Might they be trying to help someone else,
maybe even you? The goal, he reminds us, is to interpret their intentions and actions as fairly as you can.

1. Recall the last time you had an argument with a friend or family
    member. You already know your version of events. Explain the
    incident from the other person's point of view. Write a letter to
    yourself from the vantage point of the other person, describing
    their justifications and rationale.
2. List five mistakes you've made in your life. Next, bring to mind
    someone you regularly have conflict with or with whom you had
    a recent disagreement. What mistakes did they, or do they repeat-
    edly, make? Is there any overlap with your mistakes?

The Stoic Way of Life

DAY 54: TRUSTING THE HELM

We act very much as though we were on a voyage. What is possible for me? To select the helmsman, the sailors, the day, the moment. Then a storm comes down upon us. Very well, what further concern have I? For my part has been fulfilled. The business belongs to someone else, that is, the helmsman.

Epictetus, *Discourses*, 2.5, 10–11

No matter our power or position in life, we can only influence situations up to a point. Then we must relinquish control, with nothing left to do but trust that our efforts have set us up for the best possible outcome. In events where others play a role, acceptance means trusting that those we've selected to steer the ship have the wisdom and ability to lead us to clear waters.

1. When was the last time you trusted someone else fully and completely? What were the conditions that made this trust possible? If nothing comes to mind, consider the conditions you now need to relinquish control.

2. Choose one area of your life where you have partial but not total control (health, relationships, work projects, etc.). What efforts are you currently making to set yourself up for success in this area?

DAY 55: ONE THING WE KNOW FOR SURE

For I am not eternal, but a human being; a part of the whole, as an hour is part of the day. I must come on as the hour and like an hour pass away.

Epictetus, *Discourses*, 2.5, 13

Facing our own mortality is one of the hardest things we will ever do. But as Epictetus reminds us, death is part of the human condition. In fact, it's one of the few things in life that are certain. Stoic wisdom urges us to find appreciation in the enduring truth that our time here is fleeting, to learn to embrace our mortality and see it as part of a much larger story.

1. What thoughts arise when you think about dying? What happens in your body? Does it bring you comfort to consider yourself part of a larger whole?
2. Reflecting on mortality can inspire action. Write down one person you will appreciate more today, one healthy habit you will start today, and one small act of kindness you will perform before you go to sleep.

The Stoic Way of Life

DAY 56: A BEAUTIFUL LOAN

Regard it among your greatest blessings that you have had an excellent brother: you need not think for how much longer you might have had him, but for how long you did have him. Nature gave him to you, as she gives others to other brothers, not as an absolute property, but as a loan: afterwards when nature thought proper she took him back again.

Seneca, *Of Consolation: To Polybius*, 10.6

Instead of lamenting future loss, Seneca urges us to feel gratitude for the time we do have with loved ones. This philosophy extends to all types of good fortune—prosperity, growth at work, a growing family. For Stoics, the goal is to circumvent fear of loss by accepting the temporary nature of all things. Stoics choose to celebrate the beauty in this natural cycle, appreciating people and things while they are here.

1. Choose one important person in your life. Write a paragraph celebrating them. What makes them special and important to you? Express your gratitude for knowing them.
2. If you have recently lost a loved one, write a paragraph or two celebrating that person's life. How were they special and important to you? Express your gratitude for having known that person.

DAY 57: VIRTUE AS A MAINSTAY

Let it make no difference to you whether you are cold or warm, if you are doing your duty; and whether you are drowsy or satisfied with sleep; and whether ill-spoken of or praised; and whether dying or doing something else. For it is one of the acts of life, this act by which we die: it is sufficient then in this act also to do well what we have in hand.

Marcus Aurelius, *Meditations*, 6.2

For Marcus Aurelius, duty meant more than just fulfilling his obligations as Roman emperor; it also meant acting with virtue. In the Stoic tradition, each of us has a primary responsibility to be wise, just, and courageous—whether we are leading a meeting or battling an illness. Wherever we are and whatever we are doing, Stoics believe we can do it with virtue.

1. If your life ended tomorrow, how would you want to be remembered at your funeral? What steps can you take to embody that person today?
2. What is the biggest challenge you are currently facing? What does it mean to move through this challenge with a strong moral character—in other words, to live with virtue?

DAY 58: CELEBRATION AND RECOVERY

Consider which of the things that you purposed at the
start you have achieved, and which you have not; likewise,
how it gives you pleasure to recall some of them, and pain
to recall others, and, if possible, recover also those things
which have slipped out of your grasp. For people who are
engaged in the greatest of contests ought not to flinch, but
to take also the blows.

Epictetus, *Discourses*, 3.25, 1–2

1. List one thing you have accomplished in the last year. What
   makes you feel proud? How does this pride relate to your virtues?
   What is one thing you'd like to revisit—to remedy, improve, or
   make peace with? What went awry? What tools have you gained
   to better manage it?
2. Look back at your accountability goals from Day 51. How far have
   you come? Include a brief description of your progress toward
   each goal, including next steps if necessary. Follow through on
   them this week.

The Stoic Way of Life

DAY 59: AN INDIVISIBLE POINT

Throwing away then all things, hold to these only which are few; and besides bear in mind that every person lives only this present time, which is an indivisible point, and that all the rest of their life is either past or it is uncertain.

Marcus Aurelius, *Meditations*, 3.10

Marcus Aurelius reminds us that our experience of the world happens in a succession of single instants, each one an indivisible point that is always *right now*. When we accept ourselves and the world as we currently are, we can relax into what we're doing at this very moment. We learn to dwell not in the past or future but in the richness of the present moment.

1. Set a timer for five minutes. Find a comfortable seated position and relax. Observe your thoughts. Does your mind wander to the past or future? If negative emotions arise, remind yourself these are opinions, not facts. Bring your awareness back to the present moment. When the timer goes off, write down what you noticed about your experience. What did your mind do? What did you learn about yourself?
2. Write down a time you felt completely immersed in the present moment. What were the conditions that made this possible?

DAY 60: UNBROKEN CALM AND FREEDOM

An unbroken calm and freedom ensue, when we have
driven away all those things which either excite us or
alarm us . . . we thus gain an immense, unchangeable,
equable joy, together with peace, calmness and greatness
of mind, and kindliness.

Seneca, *Of a Happy Life*, 3.4

For Stoics, pain and loss are just as much a part of the human experience as are joy and satisfaction. As part of the underlying nature
of the world, they simply *are*. When we practice being with whatever
is, we are more easily able to root into our human experience within
a larger, living system. The Stoic recipe for inner peace is to find joy
internally as living beings witnessing the beauty that surrounds us.

1. Your inner conditions—your character and ability to respond
    productively to external events—lead to inner calm. How can you
    create the right inner conditions for calm? What practices and
    reminders can you build into your daily routine to keep your inter-
    nal climate just right?
2. Write down the Stoic quote that has most impacted you in the
    last 30 days. What does it mean to you? Consider making it the
    background wallpaper of your phone to return to again and again
    in the coming days.

LIVING
WITH
VIRTUE

So far, you have cultivated a Stoic mindset for living with deeper self-awareness and greater acceptance for the people and events around you. In Course C, you'll focus on how to align your purpose and values with your everyday life: to live with deeper intentionality. We'll explore the relationship between generosity and inner freedom, and uncover what integrity has to do with long-lasting happiness. At the end of your 90 days, you'll see the discipline you've developed as you head into the world more grounded, confident, just, and wise—like a Stoic.

DAY 61: FROM REACTION TO INTENTION

We must enter with brisk step upon the better course. In this kind of life there awaits much that is good to know—the love and practice of the virtues, forgetfulness of the passions, knowledge of living and dying, and a life of deep repose.

Seneca, *On the Shortness of Life*, 19.2

In ancient Greece, philosophy was seen as a therapy of the "passions," a phrase used to describe strong emotions like anger, fear, greed, envy, and so on. Yet Stoicism promises freedom from the choke hold of these emotions because of our ability to control how we respond to our environment. The result is inner peace and tranquility. Here, Seneca urges us to root into our virtues, practicing them daily so we can move away from volatile reactions and align with our deeper purpose.

1. Why do you think Seneca speaks of "practicing" virtues rather than "mastering" them? List three ways you can practice your core virtues this week.

2. How can focusing on virtue curb harmful reactions? How might this shift create space for more helpful emotions and behavior?

DAY 62: THE ART OF LIVING

Philosophy does not profess to secure for people any external possession. Otherwise it would be undertaking something that lies outside its proper subject-matter. For as wood is the material of the carpenter, bronze that of the statuary, just so each person's own life is the subject matter of the art of living.

Epictetus, *Discourses*, 1.15, 2

Ancient Stoics sometimes referred to philosophy as the "art of living": each of us is an artist sculpting our own life. The material we work with is not external goods (money, social status, career success) but our own mind and character. By using the material available to us— ourselves—we can create a work of great beauty and excellence.

1. What about your current life feels like art? Do you wish to make more of it?
2. What are the tools you use as the artist of your own life? (Examples: reading, journaling, meditation, structured routines, various mental techniques.)

_____

_____

_____

_____

_____

_____

_____

DAY 63: A DISCIPLINED ARTIST

What is your art? To be good. And how is this accomplished well except by general principles, some about the nature of the universe, and others about the proper constitution of humankind?

Marcus Aurelius, *Meditations*, 11.5

All artists must master some basic principles in order to bring energy to their creation. The art of living is no different. Here, Marcus Aurelius explains that to live well, we need a foundational understanding of human nature and our place in the cosmos. If all we can control is our response to our environment, our choices become the canvas on which we paint our life.

1. Choose one of these virtues: wisdom, justice, courage, temperance. Explain how it will guide your choices over the course of this week.

2. What virtue feels most present in your life right now? How does this virtue help connect you to the big picture, such as your place in the cosmos?

DAY 64: YOUR DAILY MINDSET

See how I eat, how drink, how sleep, how endure, how refrain, how help, how employ desire and how aversion, how I observe my relationships, whether they be natural or acquired, without confusion and without hindrance; judge me on the basis of all this, if you know how.

Epictetus, *Discourses*, 4.8, 20

Stoic ideas appeal to many, but can you put them into practice in *your* daily life? Do you keep your principles front of mind throughout the day? Are you channeling your desires away from externals and toward internal goods like wisdom and courage? For Epictetus, Stoicism is not something to apply only in times of crisis. It's a lifestyle around which to orient mindset and behavior—each day.

1. Describe what healthy Stoic virtue looks like in *your* life for each of the following situations: eating, sleeping, controlling your desires, maintaining your relationships. Identify one of these areas where you would like to grow. What would that growth look like?

2. Identify something holding you back from a goal you wish to achieve. What is your mindset around this obstacle? How does this mindset impact your behaviors?

DAY 65: LIKE AN EMERALD

Whatever anyone does or says, I must be good, just as if the gold, or the emerald, or the purple were always saying this, Whatever anyone does or says, I must be emerald and keep my color.

Marcus Aurelius, *Meditations*, **7.15**

When the people around you don't share your mindset and values, it can be difficult to make unpopular decisions. But Marcus reminds us that what other people think of our choices doesn't change who we are. An emerald is gloriously green whether anyone appreciates it or not. Like an emerald, your core elements remain the same, regardless of someone's opinions of or actions toward you.

1. Gems have an inherent color, but they can also be polished to shine brighter. What color is your character? What virtue does that hue represent? Identify two ways you can "polish" your character to show your true colors.

2. Many gemstones are known for their strength and durability. What properties do you possess that feel immovable? How can your inner strength help you shine?

DAY 66: SEEING PROBLEMS AT SCALE

The full consummation of human felicity is attained when,
all vice trampled under foot, the soul seeks the heights
and reaches the inner recesses of nature. What joy then to
roam through the very stars, to look down with derision on
the gilded saloons of the rich and the whole earth with its
store of gold!

Seneca, *Natural Questions*, introduction

Stoics remind us that we don't have to leave home for a healing experience: the sky above is always available for solace and contemplation. Amid our busy lives, it's essential to pause—and look up. By turning our gaze toward the vastness of the cosmos and the majesty of our own planet, we recognize our own limitations and see our problems at their proper scale.

1. Have you ever had an encounter with the natural world that led you to a deeper understanding of your life?
2. Set a timer for five minutes and find a place to admire the sky. What came up? Write down three or four ways you can connect with nature without leaving home.

The Stoic Way of Life

DAY 67: THE POWER OF CHOICE

That person is free who lives as they will, who is subject neither to compulsion, nor hindrance, nor force, whose choices are unhampered, whose desires attain their end, whose aversions do not fall into what they would avoid.

Epictetus, *Discourses*, 4.1, 1

Many people long to be free from constraints and obligations. We wish for more money, time, or things outside of our grasp. For Epictetus, freedom is about free will: choice. Instead of wishing for different circumstances, Stoics urge us to skillfully adapt our mindset and decisions to align with our obligations. Freedom means seizing what's always in your power: an impeccable character and honorable choices.

1. Identify a current situation where you face obligations or constraints. Can you redefine freedom as internal—the power to choose your response? What does this type of freedom look like?
2. Draw three columns. List three things you wish to change. List three corresponding virtues you can use to change them. Finally, list three corresponding decisions you can make to impact each situation.

DAY 68: WEB OF COMPASSION

The first thing which philosophy undertakes to give is fellow-feeling with all people; in other words, sympathy and sociability.

Seneca, *Moral Letters to Lucilius*, 5.4

Stoicism aims to support individuals, but at its core exist collective principles: affection, kindness, and the ability to engage with and respect others. Stoics believe that humans are naturally social animals, made to live together and cooperate. But it also distinguishes between emotional compassion, which leads to burnout, and rational compassion. When we act with rational compassion, our kindness springs from a deep and steady understanding of our kinship with other people (not from an emotional reaction). This enables us to stay strong and caring, no matter what happens around us.

1. Do you agree that we should show "fellow-feeling" to all humans, not just our family and friends? In what ways does your life touch people in other cities or other countries?

2. Describe the experience of caring for someone. Write about your affection for this person. How does your affection enrich your life?

DAY 69: CROSS-EXAMINING JUDGMENT

> Only the act which proceeds from correct judgments is
> well done, and that which proceeds from bad judgments is
> badly done. Yet until you learn the judgment from which
> a person performs each separate act, neither praise their
> action nor blame it.

Epictetus, *Discourses*, 4.8, 3

Instead of making snap judgments about the people around you,
Epictetus reminds us, remember that we usually don't have enough
information to judge accurately. Perhaps there's a justification for what
they're doing—one that you don't know about. Stoic wisdom encour-
ages us to give people the benefit of the doubt. Only if you know their
intentions can you wisely judge their actions.

1. Can you think of a time when you judged someone, only to find
   out later that you were mistaken? What judgments did you make?
   How would the situation have been different if you had refrained
   from making a hasty judgment?
2. Bring to mind a current judgment. Now let's cross-examine it. Is
   it telling the truth? What evidence reveals this judgment to be
   faulty? Call in key witnesses (like the person you've judged) and
   see what they have to say.

DAY 70: TO ADAPT IS TO LOVE

Adapt yourself to the things with which your lot has been cast: and the people among whom you have received your portion, love them, but do it truly, sincerely.

Marcus Aurelius, *Meditations*, 6.39

For Marcus Aurelius, the key to love—both inward and outward— is acceptance. Sometimes that means adapting your expectations around how you believe others should behave. When we release expectations, we not only become kinder; we also love more sincerely and experience more resilient happiness. Adaptability, in this sense, equals peace.

1. Set a timer for one minute. Think of a person you love, dwelling on their admirable characteristics and the happy experiences you've had together. What comes up? How do you feel?
2. Set a timer for one minute. Think of a person you're struggling with. Identify as many of their good characteristics as you can. Write down what they would say you are missing.

DAY 71: A SECOND LOOK AT DESIRE

People sink themselves in pleasures, and they cannot do without them when once they have become accustomed to them, and for this reason they are most wretched, because they have reached such a pass that what was once superfluous to them has now become indispensable. And so they are the slaves of their pleasures instead of enjoying them.

Seneca, *Moral Letters to Lucilius*, 39.6

Seneca reminds us of the tricky relationship between desire and unhappiness. The moment we enter a cycle of consumption—constantly craving the next thing—is the moment we lose control of our inner fulfillment. If you can't live without whatever item or experience you *have to have*, do you truly own your happiness? For Stoics, when well-being doesn't depend on luxuries, we acquire a precious freedom.

1. What have you convinced yourself you can't live without? What would your life look like if you gave it up for one week?
2. What do you habitually buy? Can you identify any patterns? How do you feel when you make the purchase? How long does that feeling last?

The Stoic Way of Life

DAY 72: TESTING YOUR RESOLVE

> Your present opinion founded on understanding, and your present conduct directed to social good, and your present disposition of contentment with everything which happens—that is enough.
>
> Marcus Aurelius, *Meditations*, 9.6

For Stoics, true contentment means being at peace with your present circumstances, no matter how much they test your strength of character. This means doing the work to accept what's happening to and around you. When we develop our reasoning ability, treat others justly, and cultivate a deep acceptance of the world's joys and tragedies, we give ourselves the power to live contently.

1. Write down one thing that's become clear to you in the past year, one compassionate action you took for someone else, and one thing that was difficult to accept but that you've come to terms with. After you write, pause, and take a moment to see how you feel.
2. Create a faux social media post where you explain to your friends that you're skipping a particular activity or purchase because you're happy with what you already have.

DAY 73: THE BUSY BAROMETER

Neither in your actions be sluggish nor in your conversation without method, nor wandering in your thoughts, nor let there be in your soul inward contention nor external effusion, nor in life be so busy as to have no leisure.

Marcus Aurelius, *Meditations*, 8.51

Stoics believe it's important to set aside time for activities that clear our minds and nourish our spirits. Sometimes that means a detox from social gatherings; other times it means sharing experiences or deep conversations with others. The key is to bring self-awareness and intentionality to this "leisure." If we're busy all the time, we risk losing touch with our barometer that tells us when we need to tap in or out. When we limit distraction, we get closer to thoughts and activities that truly fill us up.

1. Make a list of "junk food" you sometimes feed your mind. What happens when you consume too much of it? Consider the role it plays in your mental, physical, and spiritual health.
2. What leisure activities can you focus on that will cleanse your mind and renew your spirit?

DAY 74: MAINTAINING ATTENTION

> Why do you not maintain your attention continuously?
> "Today I want to play." What is to prevent your playing
> then—but with attention? "I want to sing." What is
> to prevent your singing then—but with attention? . . .
> What, will you do it worse by attention, and better
> by inattention? And yet what other thing, of all that
> go to make up our life, is done better by those who
> are inattentive?

> Epictetus, *Discourses*, 4.12, 3–5

You may have heard the adage "Where attention goes, energy flows." This is the essence of a core Stoic principle that relates attention to attitude, opinion, choice, and action. The more attention we pay to our environment and experience within it, the more intentionality we can bring to our choices. For Stoics, it's not the action that matters so much as the intentionality we bring to it.

1. Think of attention as a spotlight, illuminating its object of focus. List five things you wish to illuminate in your life. What is one step you can take toward focusing on each one?
2. When was the last time you felt completely focused on a project or activity? What were the conditions that made this attention possible?

DAY 75: NATURAL STATE OF KINDNESS

Kindliness forbids you to be overbearing toward your associates, and it forbids you to be grasping. In words and in deeds and in feelings it shows itself gentle and courteous to everyone.

Seneca, *Moral Letters to Lucilius*, 88.30

We've all been at the receiving end of someone who overasserts themselves, grasping for our love, approval, or attention. There are few things that push us farther away. Stoicism urges us to approach human interaction gently—kindness need not be loud or demanding. Humans naturally enjoy sharing time and resources. When we let this courteous attitude flow, we feel a state of calm, softly—but powerfully—benefiting the people around us.

1. Describe the last time someone was kind to you without expecting anything in return. What did this kindness allow you to do or feel?
2. Bring three people to mind whom you would like to offer your kindness. For each person, consider one subtle action you can take to make them feel appreciated or seen. Write down how you will avoid seeking their approval for this action and instead allow kindness to flow naturally and with no expectation.

DAY 76: COMPASSION AS JUSTICE

With what are you discontented? With the badness of people? Recall to your mind this conclusion, that rational animals exist for one another, and that to endure is a part of justice, and that people do wrong involuntarily.

Marcus Aurelius, *Meditations*, 4.3

Ancient Stoics believed people do wrong involuntarily. No one wants to do the "wrong" thing; rather, they believe what they're doing is right, even though it may appear misguided to us. Understanding this helps us offer compassion to those who initially annoy, frustrate, or anger us. Stoic justice dictates that we treat all humans with empathy and respect, even when we disagree with everything they do.

1. Some of the greatest political and spiritual leaders are those who have dealt peacefully with people who opposed them. Why do we admire people who treat their personal or political opponents with respect or even compassion? What does this say about their character?

2. Identify one specific person you find it difficult to be patient with. How might they believe they are doing what's right? Consider one way you can show more compassion when you remember they are doing wrong involuntarily.

DAY 77: CONTEXT IS EVERYTHING

We must remember who we are, and what is our
designation, and must endeavor to direct our actions in
the performance of our duties, to meet the possibilities
of our social relations. We must remember what is the
proper time for song, the proper time for play, and in
whose presence; also what will be out of place; lest our
companions despise us, and we despise ourselves.

Epictetus, *Discourses*, 4.12, 16–17

We all have different actions that are appropriate for us in life, based
on our circumstances, roles, talents, and character. Stoics remind
us that thinking carefully about our roles and social relationships—
keeping context front of mind—can guide us toward behavior that
others appreciate and that makes us feel proud of who we are.

1. Make a list of all the roles you hold in life. Do any of them over-
    lap? Contradict one another? How do your most important roles
    guide your choices and actions? Identify at least one recent situa-
    tion whereby your role(s) influenced your decisions.
2. Write about a time when your actions had a positive impact
    on your environment. Now consider a different situation when
    those same actions might have an adverse effect. Describe the
    conditions—the context—that shifted this outcome.

DAY 78: IDENTIFYING ROLE MODELS

> Choose a master whose life, conversation, and soul-expressing face have satisfied you; picture them always to yourself as your protector or your pattern. For we must indeed have someone according to whom we may regulate our characters; you can never straighten that which is crooked unless you use a ruler.
>
> Seneca, *Moral Letters to Lucilius*, 11.10

Stoics believe that role models provide us with a template for living well. When we don't know what to do, Stoics encourage us to ask ourselves how our role model would deal with a similar situation. Recalling a role model—a Stoic or anyone who strives to live a virtuous life—can keep us true to our principles.

1. Think back on the role models in your life, personal or public. Do you have a current role model? What virtues do these role models display? How did, or does, their life impact other people?
2. Identify a challenge you are currently facing. How would one of your role models handle this situation? What virtues would guide them (and you)?

DAY 79: THE COST OF GREED

"Yes," you say, "but the wicked person is better off." In what respect? In money; for in respect to that they are superior to you, because they flatter, are shameless, lie awake nights. What is surprising in that? But look rather and see if they are better off than you are in being faithful, and considerate. For you will not find that to be the case; for where you are superior, there you will find that you are better off than they are.

Epictetus, *Discourses*, 3.17, 2–3

When we see selfish people getting ahead in the world, it's tempting to believe there's no justice. But Epictetus flips our perspective. When people act with greed, they exchange something truly valuable (their good character) for something of no real value (material gain). When we consider the seriousness of this bargain, alignment with our values can help us rest easy at night.

1. How does your attitude toward material possessions impact your daily life and decision making?
2. Write about a situation when you preferred good character to something external like achievement, popularity, or money.

DAY 80: INTEGRITY WITHOUT FANFARE

> Don't you know that a good and excellent person does
> nothing for the sake of appearances, but only for the sake
> of having acted right?

> Epictetus, *Discourses*, 3.24, 50

Virtuous activity often happens when no one is looking. Great Stoics like Epictetus remind us that the right thing to do is the right thing to do, even if no one is there to applaud your actions. When you're tempted to do something to receive praise, Stoics remind you to act to preserve your character, not to impress or satisfy others. Virtue is its own reward.

1. Choose a role model who acted with integrity when no one understood or appreciated their actions. What values drove this person? What aspects of their character do you admire?
2. Write about a time you did something worthy of accolades but received no recognition. How did you feel? What values drove you? Would you do it again?

DAY 81: MAKING YOUR OWN LUCK

Fortunate means that a person has assigned to themselves a good fortune: and a good fortune is good disposition of the soul, good emotions, good actions.

Marcus Aurelius, *Meditations*, 5.37

Instead of waiting around for "good" things to come, Stoics urge us to make our own luck by creating goodness within ourselves. For Marcus Aurelius, *good* equates to *virtuous*, and we already know that virtue is its own reward. Even better, when we orient our emotions and actions toward wisdom, we bring a constructive energy to life that generates constructive actions for the people around us. Stoics ask a central question: which fortune will you assign to yourself?

1. What good emotions and actions do you feel full of today? At certain points throughout the next 24 hours, record when you notice this positive energy bringing you good fortune.
2. Think about a project you're working on. Identify two things you can do today to create your own luck. Can changing your mindset generate more constructive energy?

DAY 82: WHAT RULES YOU?

Hasten to examine your own ruling faculty and that of
the universe and that of your neighbor: your own that
you may make it just: and that of the universe, that you
may remember of what you are a part; and that of your
neighbor, that you may know whether they have acted
ignorantly or with knowledge, and that you may also
consider that their ruling faculty is akin to your own.

Marcus Aurelius, *Meditations*, 9.22

Marcus lists three aspects of life we should routinely examine: our mind, the universe, and the people around us. These aspects correspond to the three Stoic disciplines of logic, physics, and ethics. To live as the great Stoics, take time throughout your busy day to examine your choices and actions in all three disciplines.

1. In the past day, how have you tried to see things clearly and accurately? How often have you paid attention to your thoughts, attitude, and choices?
2. In what ways have you shown compassion to the people around you? What helps you remember that people do wrong involuntarily?
3. What connects you to the larger human experience?

DAY 83: CULTIVATING GRATITUDE

We should try by all means to be as grateful as possible. For gratitude is a good thing for ourselves, in a sense in which justice, in a sense that is commonly supposed to concern other persons, is not; gratitude returns in large measure unto itself. There is not a person who, when they have benefitted a neighbor, has not benefitted themselves.

Seneca, *Moral Letters to Lucilius*, 81.19

Seneca reminds us that the primary beneficiary of gratitude is the grateful person. When we approach social relationships—and the universe at large—with graciousness, we cultivate a sense of fulfillment and well-being. By finding new ways to be grateful, we can open new possibilities for connection and contentment.

1. Music is a great tool for tapping into emotions and building deep memories. Identify two people you want to feel more grateful toward and choose a gratitude "theme song" for them. Record how the song expresses something special about them. (Whenever you see that person, play the song in your head!)

2. How does your day shift when you express gratitude in the morning? What prevents you from doing this every day?

DAY 84: DELIGHT IN YOUR COMPANIONS

When you wish to delight yourself, think of the virtues of those who live with you; for instance, the activity of one, and the modesty of another, and the liberality of a third, and some other good quality of a fourth. For nothing delights so much as the examples of the virtues, when they are exhibited in the morals of those who live with us and present themselves in abundance, as far as is possible. Wherefore we must keep them before us.

Marcus Aurelius, *Meditations*, 6.48

Marcus Aurelius offers a convenient tool for keeping our ego in check: delight in the virtues of those around you, finding joy in their diversity. When we focus on the good qualities of those around us, we cultivate gratitude and contribute to a household or community of abundance.

1. Bring to mind someone you love. What are three of their best inner attributes? Mentally thank that person for each attribute. Now picture someone you're not as close to. Can you think of any good attributes? Mentally thank them as well, offering a friendly handshake.

2. What changes do you notice in your mindset when you consider the virtues of others? How can you experience more of this mindset?

DAY 85: FINDING YOUR FLOW

When one is busy and absorbed in one's work, the very absorption affords great delight; but when one has withdrawn one's hand from the completed masterpiece, the pleasure is not so keen. Henceforth it is the fruits of your art that you enjoy; it was the art itself that you enjoyed while you were painting.

Seneca, *Moral Letters to Lucilius*, 9.7

Over 2,000 years ago, Seneca identified the modern concept of *flow*: being completely and happily absorbed in your work. When living is our art, we can see each action as an artistic expression of ourselves. Shifting our attention away from attachment to the outcome and instead focusing on finding profound enjoyment in the action itself allows us to become deeply absorbed in the creative process of living.

1. Think about your happiest moments as a creator. Describe your experience of flow.

2. Envision a day of your life as your next creative endeavor. How will you bring a spirit of pleasant concentration to your actions as you get out of bed, brush your teeth, go to work, etc.?

DAY 86: MAKING THE MOST OF MISTAKES

> What, then? Is it possible to be free from fault altogether?
> No, that cannot be achieved, but it is possible ever to be
> intent upon avoiding faults. For we must be satisfied, if we
> succeed in escaping at least a few faults by never relaxing
> our attention.
>
> Epictetus, *Discourses*, 4.12, 19

Epictetus shows us that aiming for excellence allows us to get continuously closer to our goal, even while knowing we'll never be perfect. It's not possible to achieve complete wisdom or virtue, but that doesn't mean wisdom and virtue are unworthy goals. It comes down to attention (are we willing to bring our flaws into focus?) and intention (will this make me wiser?). If we are willing to keep working, we're on the right track to making the most of our human flaws.

1. Take one minute to write about a recent mistake you made. Read through what you wrote. Now write about this mistake while bringing more self-compassion into your retelling.
2. Consider a time you've been at fault. Was it hard to come to terms with this error? List one virtue you could bring to this situation should it, or something similar, arise in the future.

DAY 87: DON'T OVERDO IT

Philosophy calls for plain living, but not for penance; and we may perfectly well be plain and neat at the same time. This is the mean of which I approve; our life should observe a happy medium between the ways of a sage and the ways of the world at large; all people should admire it, but they should understand it also.

Seneca, *Moral Letters to Lucilius*, 5.5

When we find a helpful new mode of living, it's tempting to go enthusiastically overboard. But Seneca advises moderation, even in pursuit of a wise and healthy lifestyle. We don't want to experience burnout, and we don't want to become dogmatic. The goal is to integrate Stoicism into your life in a way that helps you live with wisdom, justice, temperance, and courage—and inspires others to do the same. Sagelike, but not isolated to a land of sages.

1. What does Seneca mean by "plain living, but not for penance"? In your life, is there any line between a simple, authentic lifestyle and unnecessary deprivation?
2. How can you go about your everyday responsibilities while practicing a lifestyle rich with Stoic virtue? What is the optimal balance for your life?

DAY 88: A SOUL RETREAT

People seek retreats for themselves, houses in the country,
seashores, and mountains; and you too are wont to desire
such things very much. But this is altogether a mark of
the most common sort of people, for it is in your power
whenever you choose to retire into yourself. For nowhere
either with more quiet or more freedom from trouble does
a person retire than into their own soul . . . Constantly
then give to yourself this retreat, and renew yourself.

Marcus Aurelius, *Meditations*, 4.3

Amid the demands of modern life, it's tempting to think a vacation
will solve our problems. And while thoughtful leisure is an important
element of Stoicism, Marcus Aurelius reminds us that there is a
fine line between intentional time to decompress and escapism from
ourselves. For Stoics, the most productive retreat is the one inward,
exposing the crevices of the soul.

1. Close your eyes and envision your own peaceful inner retreat.
   Describe in detail what you see and experience there. What is
   your mental state at your retreat?

2. When you're feeling stressed, what virtue helps you to restore
   inner tranquility? What conditions need to exist for you to be able
   to call upon this virtue during times of stress?

DAY 89: SELF-REFLECTION AS DAILY PRACTICE

I pass the whole day in review before myself, and repeat all that I have said and done: I conceal nothing from myself, and omit nothing: for why should I be afraid of any of my shortcomings, when it is in my power to say, "I pardon you this time: see that you never do that anymore"?

Seneca, *Of Anger*, 3.36

The ancient Stoic Sextius used to ask himself three questions at the end of each day: "What bad habit of yours have you cured today? What vice have you checked? In what respect are you better?" Seneca turned this into a bedtime routine, with an emphasis on unabashed honesty. For Seneca, almost more important than the questions was the truthfulness of the answers. After all, what is there to fear when you are in control of your response to everything in this world?

1. Create three journaling prompts for your nighttime ritual. Feel free to adopt or adapt from the following: *What is one thing I did well today? What is one thing I could have improved on? How will I improve tomorrow?*

2. What are three ways you will show yourself compassion rather than blame? How can you disseminate this compassion to improve the lives of those around you?

DAY 90: REPLENISHING THE GOOD WITHIN

Look within. Within is the fountain of good, and it will ever bubble up, if you will ever dig.

Marcus Aurelius, *Meditations*, 7.59

Happiness, fulfillment, and freedom are all available when we look within. In fact, there is an endless supply. No matter what's happening around us, we can tap into our inner reserves of wisdom and acceptance. It isn't easy, and it doesn't happen overnight. But if you consistently work toward inner excellence, you'll discover an evergreen source of virtue and contentment within your own mind.

1. List the inner resources you possess that you plan to call on during a rough period. How can you proactively integrate those resources into your life today?
2. Read through some of your past entries. Choose one to rip out and burn. Choose another to dog-ear to return to for inspiration or accountability. Stoicism is always a balance between nonattachment and intentionality.

CLOSING WORDS

Congratulations on completing 90 days of journaling like a Stoic.
You've reached a milestone in your life, initiating (or building upon) a
lifelong journey toward inner peace and contentment. This immersive
journaling experience was demanding, but you rose to the challenge.
Thanks to your dedication, you've already experienced some of the
psychological benefits of a consistent Stoic practice: greater purpose,
acceptance, generosity, and intentionality in everything that you do.

I hope you'll see the close of this course not as an ending, but as
a new beginning. You have everything you need to flourish. You've
cleared the ground and planted the seeds for a life of wisdom and
fulfillment. How well you tend to those seeds is up to you.

ACKNOWLEDGMENTS

Special thanks to everyone who helped make this book a reality: to the energetic team at Zeitgeist (especially Erin Nelson) for their professionalism and insight, to Chris Gill for helpful advice (on this and other projects), and to my always supportive family for their enthusiastic encouragement. I'm also grateful to my friends and colleagues in the Stoic community for their wisdom and inspiration. This book is inspired not just by ancient Stoicism, but by modern Stoicism and all those who pursue a life of virtue in our own times.

REFERENCES

Aurelius, Marcus. *Meditations*. Translated by George Long. London: Blackie & Son, 1910.

Epictetus. *"The Discourses" as Reported by Arrian, "The Manual," and "Fragments."* Translated by William Abbott Oldfather. Cambridge and London: Harvard University Press/Heinemann, 1926.

Laertius, Diogenes. *Lives and Opinions of Eminent Philosophers*. Translated by John Sellars. Los Angeles: University of California Press, 2006.

Seneca, Lucius Annaeus. *Moral Letters to Lucilius*. Translated by Richard Mott Gummere. London and New York: Heinemann/G. P. Putnam's Sons, 1915.

———. "The *Natural Questions* of L. Annaeus Seneca Addressed to Lucilius." In *Physical Science in the Time of Nero: Being a Translation of the "Quaestiones Naturales" of Seneca*, translated by John Clarke. London: Macmillan, 1910.

———. *Of a Happy Life*. In *Minor Dialogues Together with the Dialogue "On Clemency,"* translated by Aubrey Stewart. London: George Bell and Sons, 1900.

———. *Of Anger*. In *Minor Dialogues Together with the Dialogue "On Clemency,"* translated by Aubrey Stewart. London: George Bell and Sons, 1900.

———. *Of Consolation: To Polybius*. In *Minor Dialogues Together with the Dialogue "On Clemency,"* translated by Aubrey Stewart. London: George Bell and Sons, 1900.

———. *Of Peace of Mind*. In *Minor Dialogues Together with the Dialogue "On Clemency,"* translated by Aubrey Stewart. London: George Bell and Sons, 1900.

———. *Of Providence*. In *Minor Dialogues Together with the Dialogue "On Clemency,"* translated by Aubrey Stewart. London: George Bell and Sons, 1900.

———. *On the Shortness of Life*. Translated by John W. Basore. London: Heinemann, 1932.

ABOUT THE AUTHOR

BRITTANY POLAT, PhD, is a writer and researcher on Stoicism as a way of life. She is the founder of the nonprofit Stoicare, which promotes the Stoic principles of wisdom, well-being, community, and care. She is also a steering committee member of Modern Stoicism and a board member of the Stoic Fellowship, two non-profit organizations that advance public engagement with Stoicism. Brittany has a doctorate in applied linguistics but now spends most of her time sharing Stoicism worldwide through her writing, talks, and interviews.

Hi there,

We hope you enjoyed *Journal Like a Stoic*. If you have any questions or concerns about your book, or have received a damaged copy, please contact customerservice@penguinrandomhouse.com. We're here and happy to help.

   Also, please consider writing a review on your favorite retailer's website to let others know what you thought of the book!

Sincerely,
The Zeitgeist Team